COVER ART

Across the valley from the villa, Montagne Garde Grosse reaches an altitude of 944 metres. On the peak there is a telecommunications tower and a cleared space where paragliders take flight on warm summer afternoons when the thermals are rising from the valley below. The village of Nyons rests there, hemmed in and sheltered by Garde Grosse and a set of hills, from the bitter winds of the Mistral from the north and the Vent du Sud from the south. Warmer than the surrounding countryside in this microclimate, Nyons takes the nickname *'le petit Nice'*.

PROVENCE
FOR ALL SEASONS

PROVENCE
FOR ALL SEASONS

a journey

GORDON BITNEY

GRANVILLE ISLAND PUBLISHING

Copyright © 2012 Gordon Bitney

**Library and Archives Canada Cataloguing in
Publication**

Bitney, Gordon
Provence for all seasons, a journey / Gordon Bitney.

ISBN 978-1-894694-65-0
I. Title.
PS8603.I885P76 2007 C813'.6 C2007-906889-8

Editors: Christine Laurin & David Stephens
Copyeditor: Neall Calvert
Proofreader: Kyle Hawke
Book and Cover Designer: Alisha Whitley
Cover and Interior Art: Paul Dwillies
Maps: Tom Johnston

Granville Island Publishing Ltd.
212–1656 Duranleau St. Granville Island
Vancouver, BC, Canada V6H 3S4
604-688-0320 / 1-877-688-0320
info@granvilleislandpublishing.com
www.granvilleislandpublishing.com

Printed in Canada on recycled paper

This book is dedicated to
our friends in Provence.

ACKNOWLEDGEMENTS

Readers may all too easily assume that a book is the work of its author alone. This is never the case. It is always a joint effort, with each member bringing his or her special skills to the processes involved. For this book, I relied on Jo Blackmore and her team, Christine Laurin, Gerald Shuttleworth and Tom Johnston. I also owe ever so much to Marie-Hélène for her sound advice and excellent suggestions.

CONTENTS

Chapters

Appendices

NOTE

In order to preserve their privacy, I have changed the names of our friends and acquaintances in Provence.

The French words in this book have been italicized. Words that are common to both French and English are not italicized.

Provence redux

THE SUDDEN ROAR OF THE ENGINES and then the acceleration that pushed us back in our seats announced the flight was underway. By the time the plane reached cruising altitude, I was thinking through the decisions that lay ahead. Oddly, we owned the villa, even though we hadn't yet decided if we could make Provence our home for six months of each year, let alone permanently. Several years earlier, almost on a whim, we had bought the villa as a part of our retirement plans. The cultural shift was turning out to be larger than we had expected. After all, Provence has a recorded history going back thousands of years, encompassing empires that had risen and fallen, with a unique culture born out of its own struggles.

For my wife, Marie-Hélène, adjusting to France had not been very challenging, for she speaks French fluently and makes friends easily. The neighbours next door to our villa warmed to her immediately and helped her when she was there alone renovating, while I was still winding down my law practice back in Vancouver. She invited friends from Vancouver to visit and they worked together stripping wallpaper and painting.

By comparison, I felt as if I were a bit of an interloper in all this, struggling to understand the clipped and heavy French accents particular to Provence. So this year I had decided I would read about its history and travel its roads until I had made it my own.

The long-planned transition (a major passage, really) in our lives had begun once again. We had spent the winter in Vancouver and were returning to Provence early in order to experience the full transition to another season. Having spent periods of time there, we began to realize how important it had become to us. This was no longer simply a place to vacation; it had become our home in France.

* * *

I must have dozed off, for I awoke to activity around me. People were beginning to stir, lifting the small blinds that covered the windows of the jet's darkened cabin to let light in. There was a sense of peaceful awakening, of new life, of expectancy that spread across the rows of seats. The lights came on and once more flight attendants were striding the aisles, taking stock of the passengers. I could smell food being heated.

When the plane began its descent, I bent forward to look at the animal case stowed under the seat. Tabitha mewed plaintively.

"Did I hear a cat?" the woman seated in front of us, lifting her head, asked her companion.

The steel, concrete and glass structure of Frankfurt Airport was not designed for humans, rather for some efficient robots not yet invented to inhabit its sterile halls. We waited patiently for the flight to Lyon and then approached the gate.

"Vhat ist in dat case?" one of two German customs officers inquired when he saw the animal case I was carrying.

"A cat," I replied.

"Do you haf documents for dis animal?" he asked, having switched to an autocratic manner.

"Yes, I do," I said, reaching into my bag to bring out a file nearly an inch thick.

"It's just a cat," the other officer offered.

I held the file out for the first officer to examine.

"*Das ist gut,*" he said abruptly and waved us on, avoiding a morass of paperwork he didn't want to tackle.

The connecting flight was relatively short, the bright sun reflecting off the wing of the plane and into the cabin window. However, the dive through the cloud layer revealed a very different world; all colours were a muted grey and snow was blowing across the runway. After gathering our luggage, signing all the papers at the agency for the car lease and then hauling everything, including Tabitha, through the wind and snow into the agency's van, we were driven to the compound where the car was stored. There, we loaded the luggage into the car and immediately set off on the autoroute for Nyons in a blizzard.

This was not the Provence we had expected. I stayed in the right-hand, slower lane as sudden gusts of wind buffeted the car; snow hit the windshield and stuck in blobs, blocking visibility; semi-trailers highballed on by, sending up waves of slush that blinded us for seconds between sweeps of the wiper blades. My wife had been silent for some time, and I could feel her anxiety growing. Meanwhile, Tabitha meowed forlornly in the back of the car.

As we approached Valence, the traffic slowed considerably and then came to a complete stop. When it began moving again, it was a stop-start shuffle, and we managed to travel less than five kilometres in the next hour.

Then *gendarmes* stood before us on the road, guiding traffic off the autoroute onto an exit ramp. A temporary sign had been erected that read:

Attention ▶ *Déviation!*

"A detour!" I said. "The autoroute is closed."

"What do we do now?"

"I don't know. We don't have a map."

"Well, why don't we try to follow the roads that run alongside the autoroute until we reach Montélimar? That way we'll know where we are and not get lost."

"Okay. The back roads will be slow, but we should be all right."

Although the weather was getting worse, we reached Crest, a village we had visited before. The street was empty as we drove through, every shop closed, the shutters locked in place and no lights visible. On the other side of the village we saw a familiar sign pointing to Bourdeaux, and we knew the next village after Bourdeaux was Dieulefit. The headlights of the car lit the falling snow—the rest was darkness.

Intersecting roads led off in different directions. And then, instead of Bourdeaux, we came upon the village of Crupies. *Turn around and backtrack, or keep going?* We kept going, only to find that the next village was Bouvières . . . We were lost. After another discussion, it seemed sensible that if we always took the road to the right, we would find our way back to the autoroute.

We kept going, headlights on an empty road, hoping to see something familiar. But I sensed that we were well off track, and if we wound up in the mountains we wouldn't find our way out until dawn. The headlights of our car illuminated a panorama of whorling snowflakes that remained suspended momentarily in the air before dashing madly toward the windshield.

Then I saw a signpost:

Défilé de Trente-Pas ▶

The narrow defile had been carved through a hill by eons of water runoff; at one point it was just thirty paces—*trente-pas* wide. A road was built through this gorge to link one valley with another. We had driven it once in daylight and found it beautiful. The tall rock rose up next to the road that was covered with undisturbed snow. We drove beneath a long outcropping of rock that seemed to flow by us like red curtains on a moving stage, then back out into the snowfall. We were the only ones foolish enough to come this way since it had fallen. And then abruptly the gorge was behind us, and we recognized the tiny village of St-Ferréol Trente-Pas. Within another fifteen minutes we found the D94 highway leading west to Nyons.

We were approaching Nyons from the wrong direction, having strayed too far into the hills, but we were not lost on some forlorn mountain road, driving blindly in a snowstorm. As the headlights lit a road sign for Nyons, we both shifted in our seats with a heightened sense of relief. Shortly after that we saw the lights of Nyons. The storm had let up, and the last flakes floated lightly down onto an undisturbed white bed of snow.

·   ·   ·

As bright sunshine streamed into our bedroom, I got up, walked over and opened the window. The air was crisp and cold, the morning sky razor-blue. The only sound was the dripping of water from the snow melting on the trees and the rooftops. I breathed in to fill my lungs with the cold air, exhaled and then did it a second time. From the hillside perch of our villa, I could see light glint off the wet, red roof tiles in the village below. Thin tendrils of smoke rose from chimneys here and there.

Hélène got out of bed and walked over to the open window to stand beside me. She had slipped on a robe and was hugging it like a blanket. "It's beautiful, but it's so cold," she said, tightening her arms around herself.

"I've never seen snow on those peaks across the valley. Mont Garde Grosse is stunning."

"Well, at least with the heat on the house is warmer. The tile floor doesn't feel like a skating rink anymore."

Chapter 2
settling in

A CLOSED-UP AND SHUTTERED HOUSE is like a hibernating animal waiting for spring to arrive. Throwing open the shutters, opening the windows and letting in the fresh air disturbed the stillness that had accumulated over the winter months. The house responded as if awakening, blinking and stretching in the unexpected light.

After months of absence we were anxious to see if everything was still in order and if anything had gone wrong that needed immediate attention. I did a quick inspection of all the rooms and the garage and then walked around the outside of the house. Our villa was small, with the kitchen, our bedroom and the den up one floor. The exterior was ochre stucco with a tiled roof.

The garden sloped down the hillside to a road that swept in one large curve around three sides of the property. The villa's former owner, a crusty old French bureaucrat, had once been a proud gardener but had possibly lost interest after his wife had died. There were a dozen olive trees and some pines, as well as indigenous, gnarly-looking oaks and a tangle of overgrown shrubs framed by rosemary hedging that, despite our efforts a year earlier, still needed more serious attention. We had trimmed the shrubs and repaired the eroded garden paths that meandered along the slope. The olives had been picked by our neighbours in December and pruned by François, our gardener. As it was only March, there was very little greenery at all, mostly leafless limbs and branches. The rose bushes we had planted last year were among the few things still green and looked much the same as when we had left the previous fall. Nevertheless, the winter had taken its toll on an oak tree next to the road that had died.

Patches of snow remained among the trees. The neighbouring vineyards were bleak and lifeless, their bare, black stumps aligned in long rows strung with strands of wire for support. Some vines had already been pruned in preparation for the coming season, while others looked messy with the long canes still uncut from last year's growth. There was a stillness in the air as the fields lay lifeless, biding their time for the warmer weather. Only the wild almond trees with their fragrant pale blossoms offered a sign that spring was coming.

We had thought that we had left the house and yard in good condition; however, upon inspecting it after our return we realized that there was a lot more to do. The wooden gate to the driveway had not withstood the winter very well. It sagged and scraped on the driveway as the screws holding the hinges had come loose in the decayed wood. We decided to replace it with a wrought-iron gate that would have to be custom-made to fit the opening. That meant a visit to a *ferronnier*, or ironworker, who had been recommended to us. We wanted an old stone bench for the garden. And finally, I realized that I would have to edge the garden paths with stones to prevent the soil from eroding on the sloping hillside of the garden. I called François and asked him if he could deliver the stones.

While Hélène got out her pruners and set to work on the rose bushes, I decided to tackle the dead oak. My plan was to cut it down, keep some of the wood for the barbeque and give the rest to our neighbours Jean and Suzette to burn in their fireplace next winter.

On one wall in the garage hung garden tools, against another was a work bench and on the third wall was a furnace and water heater. I found the ladder, carried it out, rested it against the tree and climbed up to begin sawing off the branches. Just as I began to work, a green Citroën 2CV rattled up and braked to an abrupt stop in the middle of the road.

"*Allo, allo!*" the driver hollered out the half-open car window. It was Pierre Luc with his daughter, Violette, in the passenger seat.

"*Bonjour*, Violette," I said, waving at her as I climbed down the ladder.

She giggled and waved back at me.

Pierre Luc leapt from the car, leaving the door ajar, and walked over, his face one great radiant smile. He was already talking as I came down the ladder. "*C'est bon, c'est bon. Vous êtes arrivés.*"

"Yes, we're back for the summer, maybe longer," I said while reaching over the fence to shake his hand. He started to raise his arm and then quickly offered his left hand instead. This brought a quirky grin to his face. Then I saw why. His right hand was bandaged in white gauze.

I had gotten to know Pierre Luc last summer when his wife, Fanny, had moved to Paris with their daughter, Violette. He had been a lonely man, with only the company of his dog, Fidel. He had been unfocused and had not tended his vineyards, which may have been why his wife had left him, and he had put his property up for sale in order to follow his wife and daughter to Paris. He had never been what the French call *un homme sérieux*—a hard-working man, for he preferred to hang out at the local bars with his *copains*, or buddies. The odd jobs he took on for other people in order to raise some money were rarely finished. Then Fanny and Violette returned, and he vowed to change and rebuild the vineyards.

"What happened to your hand?"

"*Ça fait très mal*," he said, waving the bandage. "I was pruning my grapevines and almost cut my thumb off with a *sécateur*. Now I can't get my vineyard pruned before the budding starts this spring."

"Can't your *copains* from the bar help out?"

"*Non*," he said, then laughed at the suggestion.

"So what will you do?"

"*Mon oncle*—my uncle Jules—helps, but we're running out of time." He looked at the ground and then back at me. "If you're interested, I could show you what pruning a vineyard is all about."

We talked for awhile, and then he got back in the 2CV and sped on up the hill.

As I started back up the ladder, Hélène sauntered over from the other side of the house. "What was all that about?"

"He's injured his hand." I paused and then added, "So I said I'd help out."

"To do what?"

"Um . . . to prune his vines," I said casually, looking away. She turned to take a better look at me.

"Do you really want to get into that again?"

"Actually, he made it sound pretty interesting. I picked grapes last fall . . ."

"And you suffered for it!"

"I can learn what it takes to own a vineyard." I hesitated and then continued, "I could hardly say no and leave him stuck like that."

"He got you, didn't he?"

"Yeah—I guess so."

I waited for her to say something more, but she just went back to work on her roses. I was free to get back to the dead oak once more and was about to climb up the ladder when a sudden movement caught my attention. It was a cat trotting across Jean's yard straight toward me. When it reached the fence between the properties, it stopped, bounded up the tree and hopped to the ground on my side.

"*Mirteel,*" I said, pronouncing her name the French way. I bent over to stroke her head and received a throaty indulgent purr for my effort. She promptly rubbed her body against my legs and butted her head into my hand.

Last year we had rescued Myrtille and her litter from a shed which she had been accidentally locked in. Then we moved the kittens into our bedroom, where Myrtille had nursed them until fall when we carried them in their wicker basket down the hill to Yvette and Gilles, Myrtille's real owners.

I picked her up, rolled her onto her back and scratched her upturned belly, but she was too excited and pushed her way back to the ground.

"C'mon, let's go surprise Hélène."

Her purring turned into a throaty rumble, and she nudged against my legs as I walked toward the roses. "There's someone here to see you."

Hélène turned and saw Myrtille. In that moment, she stopped what she was doing, swept the cat into her arms, and they began making disgusting gushy noises at each other.

The next day I dressed warmly, found a pair of leather gloves and walked up the hill in the brisk morning air. Fidel, Pierre Luc's dog, was curled up beside him in the sun. Next to them stood an old man I immediately recognized as a caricature of a *santon*, one of those miniature *provençale* dolls. That may sound odd, but all his clothes, from his worn and faded shirt to the frayed jacket and loose pants, appeared to hang on him as if he had shrunk inside his very clothing. From a strap over his shoulder hung a miniature wooden keg. I had heard that men once filled these kegs with wine to drink while working in the vineyards. He had the weathered appearance of someone who had lived a life outdoors.

"*C'est mon oncle* Jules," Pierre Luc said, introducing us.

All the man said was "*Eh bheng*"—yet he stared sharply at me for a brief second before glancing away. I felt he had taken a measure of me.

By contrast, Pierre Luc couldn't have been more open and willing to engage in conversation. And he was all smiles now. He motioned for us to follow him over to the vineyard, where he stopped beside a row of vines. One look was all it took to see the tangle of overgrown canes from several years of neglect.

"I don't have money to buy those new power *sécateurs*," Pierre Luc said. "So we do it the old way—by hand . . . maybe next year. I had to buy a truck for now—anyway, a power one would have lopped it right off." He made a flicking motion as if something was flying from his bandaged hand. . . . With the cane now pointed at one of the vines, he said, "The old wood with the bark on it doesn't need pruning. But the cane has to be pruned and then tied to the wire." He made a quick cut and winced, holding the *sécateur* clumsily in his bandaged hand. "*Ici, commencez ici*—start here. Leave three or four leaf nodes on the old cane." Then he handed me the *sécateur* and said, "*Vous, maintenant.*" It was my turn. He put two forefingers on another cane, "*Ici.*"

"*D'accord*," I said in agreement and cut the cane where his fingers had been.

"*D'acc*," he said, clipping the extra vowel.

The work was similar to harvesting grapes last fall, but easier since I could stand erect instead of bending over to reach the grape clusters hidden below the leaves.

Pierre Luc must have felt he had done all he could, for he smiled and said he would come back later. Then he waved his bandaged hand and walked toward the house with Fidel at his side. The *santon* doll and I were left standing in the vineyard.

No sooner was Pierre Luc a short way off than Jules snapped, "*Pas d'acc!*—Ignore him. He knows nothing." Then he began talking very quickly in a staccato delivery that ran all the words together into one hard burr. He must have seen the confusion on my face, for he stopped and with the *sécateur* in his hand, began to show me where and how to cut the canes. "*Comme ça, et comme ça,*" he said, measuring along the cane from the hard wood of the trunk and making several swift cuts. He was not nearly as generous as Pierre Luc, for he left just two nodes on each cane.

We started working just a few feet apart. He moved with a rhythmic intensity, eyeing a vine quickly then lopping off the overgrowth of cane and tying the remaining cane to the wire trellis for support. Then he moved to the next vine and repeated the process. I tried to keep up with him but lacked his discerning eye and practised skill. My hands, even with gloves, felt stiff in the cold morning air, and rubbing them together from time to time didn't help. Every so often Jules would come back, look at my work and give advice. I was learning, although slower than I would have liked.

When I walked down the hill at the end of the day, I no longer saw any romance in wine-making. It was mind-numbing, tedious work. But also I had a weary sense of having accomplished something.

"So how did it go?" my wife asked as I opened the door and walked in.

"It will take two more days," was all I said.

Two days later, in the mid-afternoon sun, Pierre Luc, Jules and I sat with a glass of wine on the south side of his stone house. Jules silently smoked a home-rolled cigarette that he pinched between his thumb and index finger. With the pruning done, Pierre Luc had become loquacious.

"I can relax and wait for the budbreak."

He saw my inquiring look.

"Oh—that's when the first growth shows up on the canes. After that the new canes shoot out, the leaves open and little clusters appear. They look like tiny grape clusters, but they're just flower buds. The flowers open, the bees do their work and then the grapes set." He smiled and took a sip of wine. "Spring is an expectant time of year, like the early stages of a pregnancy, when winter is behind and the growth of summer lies ahead.

"I never wanted vineyards. As a child, I watched my father lose heart when the Viognier variety of grapes he planted was a big flop. Nobody bought his wine. After his death, I just let the vineyards go. But now look at it," he said with a sweep of his arm. "Viognier has become popular and is beginning to sell well—and I have lots of it. All I need is a good year and I can pay back the bank.

"Come, look here," he said, standing up and motioning for me to follow. "See there at the top of the slope how the vines are smaller up there. That's because the top drains first and the vines get less water. Down lower you can see the vines are bigger and can produce more fruit."

He turned to look at me. "The colder air gathers at the bottom of the hill. Worse, in wet weather the roots sleep in the water and we get disease and rot. Each vine, each row is different, growing, maturing and yielding different grapes."

I listened, beginning to get some idea of the challenges a *vigneron* had to deal with. Even with all the modern knowledge, the problems remained fundamentally the same—the land and the weather. And even though I had no vines, I was in the middle of wine country, and I wanted to know what it took to make the wines I enjoyed so much.

Pierre Luc was displaying an optimism that I hadn't heard before. There was none of the despondency that I had seen last summer when his wife had left with Violette and he had been living alone. Their return in the fall had changed him. All the same, I knew that he hadn't tended a vineyard, made wine or ever worked at anything.

When I returned home, I told Hélène about the day's work and what Pierre Luc had said. "He didn't do a minute's work with us and has never tended a vineyard."

"You've read Tom Sawyer?"

I stared at her, but she had turned her back and continued ironing. I felt troubled by all of this because I sensed that Pierre Luc was divided between his family responsibilities and his lazy ways with his old chums who hung around the Bar des Amis.

Chapter 3
truffling ~ dog tales ~ cycling for croissants

WE DECIDED TO GO into Nyons for the outdoor morning *marché* that has been held every Thursday for centuries. It was small at this time of year, with only the most diehard merchants in attendance, dressed in heavy winter coats to fend off the cold, stamping their rubber boots on the ground and rubbing their hands together. Their faces were ruddy, and as they talked their breath sent puffs of mist into the air as if their words were visible. The couple that sold roasted chicken were more fortunate as they could bask in the heat of their rotisserie where banks of chickens turned on skewers. We shared in the warmth while Hélène reacquainted herself with *madame* and bought one hot off a skewer.

By noon, the regulars were gathering at La Belle Époque and already the *bistrot* looked busy.

"*Bonjour, Monsieur/Dame!*" the owner's wife smiled warmly.

"*Bonjour, Madame.*"

"*Comment allez-vous?*" she asked.

"*Bien, merci. Et vous?*"

Then her husband came over to shake our hands and lead us to a table.

The *menu du jour* posted on the chalkboard on the wall read: '*escalope de veau avec sauce blanche*'. We both ordered the veal, and when the plates arrived at the table the waitress turned out to be our friend Alice from the nearby village of Vinsobres.

"You're still here!" Hélène exclaimed. "I thought you were moving back to Quebec."

"*Oui, oui.* That is true. But it didn't work out. Here, my parents can look after my daughter while I earn some money. She will start school next year. Excuse me, I'll come back. The boss wants my help." And she headed off to serve other tables.

Every now and then she stopped at our table to get in a few more words. As we left, Alice waved at Hélène and held one hand up to her ear.

"I'm to call her tomorrow, and we'll get together to catch up on things. I think she's met someone . . ."

When we opened the door of the house, the telephone was ringing. Hélène moved quickly to answer it.

"*Bonjour,* Suzette!—*Oui, oui. Nous sommes arrivé dans la tempête hier soir.—Oui! C'était terrible. . . .*"

Hélène had adopted the clipped *provençal* accent, so I gave up listening and went back to the bedroom to finish unpacking my suitcase. A few minutes later I got a summary.

"That was our neighbour, Suzette. She knew we were driving in last night and was worried when we didn't arrive on time. She says we were lucky. The TV5 news announced that a semi-trailer had jackknifed on the A8 Autoroute and several people died. She thought we might have been involved. Oh, and with all the fresh snow Jean wants to go skiing in the Alps. Are you interested?"

"Yes, but I am going truffling with Marcel tomorrow."

I had jumped at the chance to actually see how a dog finds truffles, and I wanted to dig one out with my own hands and smell its earthy, pungent aroma. A truffle, however, is a fungus like the mushroom that matures in the fall and raises its cap above the ground to send spores into the air. A truffle never breaks the surface, remaining out of sight while it matures during the winter.

Marcel lived in Bouchet and was one of those self-contained, hardy farmers who knew how to live off his land and within his means. Even though he accepted the government grants that had become a way of life to so many French farmers, he remained cautious and preferred to be self-reliant, guarding his privacy and independence. He was one of those people who typically lived their entire lives in the village or on the land where they were born. They rarely visited other nearby villages unless they had business there, were hard-working and never asked favours from anyone. Each family had to (and was even proud to) subsist on the resources available. And in turn, each community would rely on its members unless it was absolutely necessary to seek help from another community. To use a tradesman from another village was viewed as a serious breach of solidarity.

The next day I drove over to meet Marcel. When I arrived he was already standing at his front door. It was early and a cold wind blew the low, grey clouds overhead.

"It's been wet and muddy. Not good conditions for the dog to pick up scent."

He called his dog, which came around the corner of the house at a run. When it saw me, it stood off and barked aggressively. He patted it on the head and the dog settled down again.

"Truffling dogs are valuable and are often stolen," he said, grimacing. "I lost a good dog once, so I've trained this one to bark at strangers."

We got in my car and, with the dog between Marcel's legs, drove to a wooded hillside where he pointed to a spot to park. The dog jumped out of the car and turned to Marcel, wagging its tail with expectation.

As we began walking into the scrub oak trees, our boots made squishy sounds on the ground that was soggy from the recent snowfall.

"She won't truffle if she feels I'm not paying attention. She does it to please me. It's like a game to her. When she finds one, I have to reward her with attention and a treat of some sort. If I were to ever beat her, she would never again truffle for me."

The dog began sniffing at the ground ahead of us. Every now and then she looked back to make sure Marcel was following, then went on with the hunt again. Nothing much happened; so we walked deeper into the woods. After about half an hour the dog still hadn't found anything.

"I think she feels I'm neglecting her. Let's you and I stop talking and I'll just talk to her. Maybe that will get her on track."

We walked some more through the scrub oak trees and undergrowth, letting the dog lead the way.

"*Bien, bien,*" he cooed as if talking to a baby. This seemed to kindle a spark in the dog and it began sniffing more earnestly. Then it stopped and started energetically pawing at the ground. Marcel walked over, bent and stroked the dog's head, talking to distract it from further digging. He reached into a pocket of his windbreaker and gave the dog a tidbit to eat. Next he pulled a small garden trowel from his other pocket. After loosening the soil, he dug his free hand into the mud, brought up a handful and filtered it through his fingers. He was left with a few round stones that he picked through and tossed away, until several lumps remained in his hand.

"Here," he said, "smell this . . . It's small . . . but it's a good one." He passed it over to me.

I took it and sniffed, smelling moist earth but also the telltale pungent odour of the truffle. It was hardly the size of a large marble, covered in pale earth with the dark brown colour of the truffle showing through.

"This one's bigger," Marcel said, brushing the mud off another one and handing it to me. "Some people call it a *diamant noir*—a black diamond. Others call it a smelly lump of coal. Do you see that there is no grass growing under that tree?" He made a sideways glance at a tree to indicate that I should follow his gaze. "Truffles feed on the roots and take over the ground. That's why it's so barren there."

He put the truffles in a small sack, then bent over and lavished affection on his dog again, petting its head and rubbing its sides. Then he pointed at the trees. The dog seemed to understand the gesture, for it went in that direction, sniffing the ground, stopping only to see if Marcel was following.

By mid-afternoon we had returned to Marcel's house with a good handful of truffles in his sack. "We'll wash them and dry them." He emptied the contents on the kitchen table and looked them over. "You are with us for dinner, *non?*"

"Well, Hélène is at home and . . ."

"*Excellent!*" He said, now grinning while scrubbing the truffles in the sink and depositing them one by one on a dry cloth before returning them to the sack. "My wife wants to meet you both, and she has dinner all planned. Here," he said, handing me the sack. "*Ce sont pour vous*—these are yours. I can get more another day." He held it out to me.

This was clearly a 'don't refuse or risk insulting him' situation. I took the sack and thanked him.

"At seven o'clock then," he said, leading me to the door.

On a cold winter night, the country dinner was almost intoxicating. Marcel's gruff exterior seemed transformed around his family. They welcomed us into their home, and his wife and their two children showed a genuine happiness and contentment with life. For people working hard to make a living on their farm, they showed a generosity that left us feeling like best of friends, friends who had known each other for years. There was a camaraderie which warmed us with its honesty.

Two mornings later, Jean backed his old Renault down his driveway behind our house and I walked out with a ski suit, gloves and toque in my arms. The two of us had decided to drive several hours into the mountains past Serres to Montagne du Loup. The weather had warmed and the snow was slushy and difficult, so we skied ourselves to exhaustion and then arrived back late in the afternoon of the third day.

I was thinking about dropping into a comfortable bed when Hélène looked at my dishevelled, unshaven state and pushed me toward the shower.

"Suzette has invited us to dinner tonight. You've got half an hour to clean up and get dressed."

I did as I was told.

Jean, in his seventies, was a good ten years my senior and, as he walked down his driveway to greet us, he looked refreshed and ready for the evening. He had outskied me, and I was the worse for wear in trying to keep up. Rest was about the only thing that interested me at this point.

Suzette's dinner was wonderful and gave us a chance to catch up on the news of the winter. After a lot of talk Hélène raised both her hands in mock drama.

"Last night I awoke to a cat screeching outside. It was so loud I thought something awful had happened. So I got out of bed and looked out the window. Of course I couldn't see anything, but the screeching got louder than ever. I put on my slippers and went outside. I couldn't tell what was going on, but I could see that Tabitha was up a tree by the gate. So, with great difficulty, I got the ladder out and carried it over, put it against the tree and climbed up to rescue her. Just then a car came up the road. There I was in nothing but my nightie and fluffy slippers on a cold winter night halfway up a tree, caught in the headlights of a car! And even worse, the driver stopped, got out and asked if I was all right. All I could say was that I was fine, thank you. I guess he saw my embarrassment because he just smiled at me and then got back in his car and drove off."

Suzette and Jean burst out laughing. I stared at Hélène. She blushed.

"Tabitha was fine. I'll bet everyone in Nyons knows about me by now."

"Let me tell you a story we heard this winter," Suzette said. "Two elderly couples who had known each other for years would get together regularly for dinner. Their children were grown and away from home; so to fill the emotional gap created by their departure, both couples had acquired pets.

"The one couple—who I'll call '*Monsieur/Dame* X', for I can't use their names—were cat fanciers. The other couple— who I'll call '*Monsieur/Dame* Y'—preferred lapdogs and had a miniature Chihuahua. It went everywhere with them, even to their friends' house one night this last winter. The plan was to have apéritifs there and then go out to a restaurant. One thing led to another and after more than just one *apéro* they were ready to leave for the restaurant but both pets were asleep, the cat curled up on the couch and the dog on a deep cushioned armchair next to one of its owners. So they left them.

"Dinner was a great success, and by the time they left the restaurant it was quite late. Arriving home they found the front door ajar. After checking the house for possible burglars, the only thing missing was the miniature Chihuahua. The cat was asleep on the couch where they had left it. They searched the house a second time and then the garden as best they could in the dark of night, but the dog was not found. Finally they gave up, and *Monsieur/Dame* Y went home without their dog.

"The next day the search commenced again but with no better result. Then, weeks later, when *Madame* X was cleaning house, she swept the broom under the sofa and along with the dust she found a small, wiry curve of beige hair. She picked it up, examined it and then looked at her cat that was sleeping peacefully on the couch. 'Oh, *Minou!*' she said. Eventually *Monsieur/Dame* Y acquired another dog, and everything settled back to normal once more."

"Is that really true?" Hélène asked, shocked.

"Well, apparently it was a *very* big tom," Suzette replied. "Shall we have dessert?"

.   .   .

We were now settling into our normal routine each morning, Hélène making coffee while I drove into Nyons to buy the daily edition of the *International Herald Tribune* as well as fresh croissants. I knew that the *boulangère* made only enough croissants to satisfy the daily demand and no more, so I had to set off early each day. It was about one kilometre from our house to the main square of Nyons, just far enough so that I didn't want to walk, yet ridiculously close to use the car, but all the same I drove.

It was busy as I stepped inside the *boulangerie*, and the waiting *Nyonsais* looked me over one by one before looking away again. I was *l'étranger*—the outsider in their midst. So much for blending in, I thought, as I waited in the crowded space between the door and the counter. The air was permeated with the smell of freshly baked goods and heavy with moisture. The windows were fogged over and there was a constant rustling-of-paper sound: bags being stuffed with pastries; breads being wrapped with bits of paper to cover the centre part of the loaf and not the ends.

"*Cinq euros, trente!*" the lady *boulangère* behind the counter snapped out, as if to move on to another customer.

When my turn came I had already had time to practise in my mind the words I needed to use, and so I said "*Quatre croissants, deux pains-au-chocolat et une baguette, s'il vous plaît.*"

"*Les beurres ou non?*" she fired back at me.

"*Les beurres,*" I said. I had forgotten that croissants at this *boulangerie* were available either with extra butter or '*normale*'.

She filled the paper bag while I pulled a crumpled ten-*euro* note out of my pocket and put it on the glass countertop.

"*Merci, madame,*" I said, picking up my change and the paper bag.

"*À demain,*" she said, acknowledging that I would be back the next day. I smiled at her and then wove my way past waiting customers to get to the door. Tomorrow she would bake more croissants, knowing that her sales had just increased by one more household.

After some days of driving into the village for croissants, one morning I dressed in warm clothes, found a pair of gloves, pumped up the tires and rolled my all-purpose bike out of the garage. I pushed it down the driveway and then started off quickly pumping the pedals to build up body heat against the cold morning air. I accelerated down the hill and around the first wide bend, then braked hard for the switchback at the bottom of the hill, all the while weaving back and forth dodging potholes. I crossed the bridge over the stream and reached the outskirts of the village, passing first the Intermarché, where we shopped for food, and then the old terminus of the railway line that had long since disappeared from the landscape. At the *tabac presse* I stopped to buy the *Trib* and then pedalled slowly through the walled arcade and out the other side to the *boulangerie*. The patrons looked me over once again, taking in my arctic clothing as I peeled off my gloves.

The ride back to our villa felt good to start with, but by the time I had pumped and puffed my way back up the hill like a small steam engine, I felt ridiculously tired. Still, it had to be better than driving and could only get easier as my conditioning improved. After the effort of the ride I noticed the coffee tasted richer than usual.

Chapter 4
the welcome blossoms of spring

Is it so small a thing
To have enjoyed the sun,
To have lived light in the spring . . .

AGRICULTURE REMAINS the economic base; it forms the way
of life in Provence. The seasons—*printemps, été, automne*
and *hiver*—are the real measures of each year, not the weeks
and months created for a calendar. For farmers, life revolves
around the seasons, and each one brings a different set of
tasks and new rewards.

With the approach of spring, the sun rose noticeably
earlier each morning and lasted longer into the evenings.
The warmer weather brought renewed activity and colour to
the fields. Grass began to grow again beneath the trees in the
orchards. Blossoms appeared first on the almond, followed by
the apricot and then the cherry. The rows of grapevines in the

vineyards lost their black gnarled look as the leaves unfurled. Birds returned. Spring affected the villagers as well—smiles came more naturally, along with more sonorous *bonjours*. Everyone moved with a relaxed new vigour. There was a new quality to the air. Shop doors were propped open, allowing the smell of baked goods and coffee to filter out onto the streets.

One day asparagus arrived at the Thursday market. We had already seen the long rows of plastic in the fields covering the new spears to keep them white and tender. Bundles were piled high on the tables according to size, from thick and stubby to long, thin tendrils, their white tips sometimes tinged pale purple. They were still muddy from the fields, like the earth-stained hands of the ruddy-faced farmers who had cut and brought them to the market. We stopped at a stall to talk to woman who was still wearing her rubber boots, and bought a kilo for the week, knowing that the best asparagus would not be available for long.

"It grows so fast we have to cut it quickly," she said, "before it shoots up and goes to seed." She held a thick spear upright in her fist as if to demonstrate its quality. "It is at its best very young."

•   •   •

Our gardener, François, who had been recommended to us by friends, began to look after the tasks that we couldn't do ourselves. During our winter absence, he had cleaned up the garden and pruned the olive trees. He was not a tall man, and although he was muscular, he did not look particularly athletic. When I shook his hand the first time we met, I learned he was also very fine-boned. By any standard, he should not have been as strong as he was. All the same,

I watched him take on tasks that I would have avoided. Once, when a tree trunk that was over a foot in diameter had to be removed, he skilfully used a hatchet, the only tool available.

He was an exceptionally self-effacing, almost shy, person who always wore a smile that was as genuine as his willingness to see a job to completion. His other skill was correcting my French. In other words, he often worked on both me and the garden at the same time.

One day while we were unloading the stones for the garden path off his truck, another truck drove up with the stone bench I had bought at the used materials yard. A man got out to confirm that they were at the right house, while the other man parked the truck. Then the two deposited the bench along with its two pedestals in the middle of the driveway.

"Can you move it to the other side of the house?" I asked.

"That's not our job," one of them said, got back in the truck and waved as they drove away.

François and I looked at the bench lying in the driveway. I attempted to lift one end and quickly realized it was too heavy for me to move.

"*Pas de problème*"—no problem, François said. He climbed onto the back of his truck, where he extricated a two-wheeled handcart from among his gardening tools and then handed it down to me. Next, he hopped down and proceeded to work the bench onto the cart; together we towed it across the gravel patio to the other side of the house. We set the pedestals into the ground and then, in one joint effort, heaved the bench into place.

My wife had been watching from where she was gardening and walked over with her pruning shears in her gloved hand.

"Wow! Does it ever look good in front of that stone wall. All we need now is a clump of lavender at each end. When it blooms this summer, it'll be awesome!"

We all stood back admiring our success when Tabitha walked over, rubbed her chin against the bench and then hopped on to it, as if laying claim to this new object.

Light rain settled in that afternoon, so we stayed indoors to do some household tasks and relax. My wife was reading M.F.K. Fisher's translation of Brillat-Savarin's treatise *The Physiology of Taste*, and I was working on my French with a Georges Simenon mystery.

Tabitha had hopped onto the sofa, curled up on my lap and gone to sleep.

"This is interesting," Hélène said. "He says that a dinner should move from the most substantial courses to the lightest, while the wines should move from the lightest to the headier and more aromatic."

"That makes sense," I said, and went on reading.

"Wow, is he keen on cheese! Listen to this: 'A dinner which ends without cheese is like a beautiful woman with only one eye.' What a brutal comparison!"

"Ugh," was all I said, trying to focus on the mystery again. However, the bizarre nature of the comparison stuck in my mind. "Would you like some tea?"

"That would be nice," she replied, without lifting her head from her book.

As I got up, I moved Tabitha from my lap onto the sofa. By the time I had put the kettle on, Tabitha was curled up on the warm spot where I had just been sitting. I picked her up and put her on my lap. When the kettle came to a boil,

I moved her again, and once again she settled onto my warm spot on the sofa. This time as I returned Tabitha emitted a grumble and hopped onto the floor. I picked her up and put her back on my lap.

"Aren't you going to pour the tea?"

"Tabitha won't let me. Maybe you can."

She poured two cups of tea and put one next to me.

Instead of returning to her book, she reached for the morning *Trib* and began scanning the pages. Then she laughed. "Here's an ad in the Personals section. A woman wants to meet a mature man. She gives quite a flattering description of herself and then states that the man she is looking for must be '*pas de pantoufle*'! He can't be an old man wearing slippers!"

"I don't quite get it."

"It's a French expression for a man who just shuffles around the house and doesn't do anything. She wants someone young, not an old fart."

That evening I was setting the table for dinner when Tabitha came in and sat by her empty food bowl. She looked at me while I set the table, then she meowed. I ignored her; she meowed again and didn't take her eyes off me. I continued with what I was doing. Finally she walked over, wound herself between my legs, meowed and returned to her food dish.

"In a minute, Tabitha," I said.

"She wants to be fed."

"I'm getting a bottle of wine from the cellar. Then I'll feed her."

I walked away, but Tabitha dashed after me, batted at my leg, bit my ankle and then ran off.

"Ouch!" I said. "Why did she do that?"

"You didn't feed her."

I opened a can of cat food, spooned some into a bowl and put it on the floor. We were at the table having dinner when Tabitha walked back into the kitchen. She ignored her food bowl and sat on the floor beside me. Then she reached up with one paw and patted at my wrist.

"She's poaching. Don't spoil her."

I gave her a bit of meat from my plate and she ate it. Then she walked over to Hélène, reached up and patted her on the wrist. Hélène muttered something and then picked a bit of meat off her plate and held it out. Tabitha nipped at it to pull it out of her fingers and let it drop to the floor, where she ate it and asked for more.

"*Merde*," Hélène said.

At that moment Myrtille announced her presence with an owlish Siamese meow, followed by vigorously rubbing herself against my leg. Next she went to check out the food bowl and ate what Tabitha was now ignoring. Tabitha watched Myrtille and then reached up and patted Hélène's hand once more. A détente between the two cats had been reached last summer, but there were still territorial rivalries that surfaced in short skirmishes. Tabitha had staked out the sofa as her space. All the same, Myrtille would walk by, rubbing her tail along the cushion that Tabitha was sleeping on, as if testing the exact boundary. Then she would walk away to curl up on the seat of one of the wicker chairs that was pushed under the kitchen table.

A few days later we were washing up the dishes after dinner when Myrtille reappeared in the olive tree and hopped onto the balcony to stand at the open French doors to the kitchen. She didn't come in. *Odd*, I thought, as I got on with what

I was doing. Then she turned and walked back over to the edge of the balcony where she meowed and sat looking down the tree.

Hélène stepped onto the balcony to the railing to see what this was about. "She's not alone."

I came out. At the base of the olive tree were two young cats, not kittens any longer, but not yet grown to their full size. One after the other, not having acquired the full agility and assurance of adult cats, they clawed their way clumsily up the tree and onto the balcony.

"She's brought her kittens for us."

Hélène put a bowl of cat food on the floor. They walked over and ate, pushing and shoving at each other. Myrtille, who last year had what could be called a competitive appetite, just sat nearby and watched. The two young ones stayed long enough for us to pick them up, pet them and then put them down next to Myrtille, who watched every movement. Finally, she led them back down the olive tree. That was the only time she showed us her kittens; she did not bring them around again. She seemed to treat our house as her time away from them—a mother tired of the demands of her offspring.

*　　*　　*

Every Frenchman seemed to own *un vélo* and ventured out regularly, either alone or in groups, spinning in swarms along the roads. Cars inevitably lined up behind, waiting impatiently yet politely for any straight stretch of road to pass. My *vélo*, an all-purpose bike with fatter tires to accommodate rougher roads, had become a companion of sorts. If I stopped riding for more than a day or two, I missed the exercise and was anxious to get back to it once again.

One morning, as I rode into the village, I saw the owner of the bookstore, the *librairie*, putting out a stand of road maps, so I stopped and went in. L'Institut Geographique National of France (IGN) published a blue series of 1:250,000 scale maps for every region of the country. When I unfolded the map covering our village, I was surprised at the detail. I could make out even the smallest lanes and trails as well as a black rectangle that indicated our villa. This was a treasure of information for back-road cycling, so I bought maps for all the surrounding areas.

The IGN maps led me and my bike in the ensuing months down lanes and shortcuts to places along meandering routes I never dared to take the car—even to tiny hamlets at the end of remote trails that only the residents drove and few people knew existed.

The new activity of biking that I had taken up on returning this spring was both physically rewarding and mentally stimulating. Riding gave me time to think about the culture of Provence. It was still an exotic place for me, where formal rituals and cultural differences often crept up unexpectedly. At first they seemed subtle and minimal: another language, one that was manageable with effort; the strict formality of greeting someone; rigid restaurant hours with no place open to eat between breakfast and lunch, and between lunch and dinner, unless a McDonald's had made an unwanted inroad into a village. It was as if the very view of the world in Provence was different from that in Canada. Workers going out on strike at any opportunity and staying out until the country reached the brink of economic meltdown and social chaos was considered normal. The more I learned, the more small things eluded me.

Walking my bike into the garage late one morning, I found Hélène stretching after one of her runs.

"So where did you ride today?" she asked.

"To the east. First to Les Pilles along the D94 and then south on the D185 to Châteauneuf-de-Bordette behind Montagne Garde Grosse. I came out of the hills near Mirabel-aux-Baronnies and then took the D538 back." I said this rather matter-of-factly, although my pride must have been showing.

"That's great. You're getting to know those roads."

"Col de la Croix Rouge is back there, and it's a bugger to climb—almost a mountain pass. The road runs over a steep ridge between two valleys. There's a church with a big red cross at the top in the middle of nowhere. It's stunning in there—rugged and lonely as hell. I don't know how people a hundred years ago eked out a living on those barren hillsides; yet there are stone farmhouses up there with no running water or plumbing. They have electricity and TV dishes, but those may be the only concessions to modern life. I actually rode by an old woman who was leading her donkey with a load of firewood on its back."

"You're losing weight," Hélène said.

"Yes, I guess I am. That was my 'office weight', from sitting at a desk all day." I certainly felt trimmer. Then I glanced at her physique, lean from running every other day. She saw my admiration and smiled.

Chapter 5
budbreak and other things ~ where to meet the locals

As SPRING ADVANCED, the weather improved along with my stamina, allowing me to me to venture out farther afield. I also noticed that my body felt uncomfortable when I missed a ride. I was becoming addicted to physical exercise. Some days I rode in the direct hot sun, while other days the shadows of clouds chased me over the landscape. I even went out in wet weather, wearing simply a waterproof jacket; the energy I expended kept me warm. Facing into the wind could change everything, making an easy stretch of level road like an uphill ride until I finally tired, turned around and, with my clothes flapping around me in the breeze, let the wind help carry me home.

By mid-April budbreak was well underway in the vineyards and the tight clusters of flowers would soon be replaced by grape bunches. This was a risky time of year, for a late frost could easily damage the flowers before the grapes had a chance to set. The apricots had already successfully flowered, despite a close call with the late snowfall.

Pierre Luc had invited me over to talk about the growing season ahead and show me how his vineyards were coming along. We talked for several hours while walking the rows that I had helped prune a month earlier. As he spoke his pride showed, and I was his willing audience, learning about vineyards and winemaking. His wife, Fanny, had attended l'Université du Vin just after they were married. He had given up on the vineyards, and when their daughter, Violette, was born, he tried working at odd jobs around the area to earn money.

Pierre Luc's father had taken a risk by planting the Viognier variety of grapes in his vineyard, as well as the vineyard he leased from a neighbouring friend. Unfortunately, Viognier was relatively unknown, and when his wines wouldn't sell he gave up and simply sold the grapes at rock-bottom prices to the cooperative for blending into common *vin de pays* wine. After his father died, Pierre Luc did little with the vineyards until Fanny returned with Violette after their short separation.

One day I saw Jean up on his roof. When I asked him about it he said that he was checking to see if any roof tiles had cracked and needed replacing. He suggested I do the same. So I propped a ladder against the house and climbed up. Creeping cautiously to the crown of the roof, I straightened up briefly and looked around at the village below and the surrounding mountains. Mont Garde Grosse dominated impressively across the valley. Heights were never something I cared for, so I bent over again and, feeling like a cat-burglar wearing a pair of old runners, began crawling around on all fours to avoid slipping and becoming a poster-boy for a safety commercial.

The wood or asphalt shingles of Canada couldn't withstand the summer sun of Provence; much more durable products were needed. The old classic Roman tile was the norm and came in assorted shapes and sizes. In French the word is *tuile* and in Latin *tegula*. The tiles were generally fifty centimetres long by twenty to twenty-five centimetres wide, and curved down the length. A bottom course was laid with the concave surface facing up and overlapping as they ran up the roof. The top course was laid with the convex side facing up to drain the water into the trough of the bottom course. The result was a system that was amazingly simple and easy to repair.

Early tiles were made from fired clay that was a natural brownish-red colour, hence the name *terracotta* tiles. Nowadays they are made of concrete with artificial red colour added. Variations evolved over time. For instance, our roof used an S-shaped product that incorporated the bottom and top course in one tile. In a hot climate, this allowed the air to circulate freely around the tiles, helping to disperse the heat of the sun. One look in the attic revealed a complex system of beams, rafters and struts to support all the weight.

I was beginning my inspection by checking the tiles along the edge of the roof when butterflies suddenly took flight in my stomach. Crawling about two and a half storeys above the ground was not the best activity for a person with a touch of vertigo. I pulled back from the edge and went to work lightly tapping the tiles with a small hammer, listening for the ring of a whole tile or the flat discord of something cracked or broken.

It took time to cover the roof, but only two needed replacing. Luckily, the former owner had left a cache of extra tiles in the garden shed, so I carried them, one by one, up the ladder and across the roof. However, the repair required more ingenuity than I had anticipated; it required prying up the surrounding tiles, pulling out the broken one and then sliding the new tile into place, all without breaking the adjacent tiles. Once this was done, I made a final check.

Where two roof angles intersected, I noticed that the lead trough had weathered and cracked. This looked bad enough from the outside; but when I checked in the attic, water had been leaking in for so long that a supporting beam was seriously rotted. This repair was beyond my skills, and by the time a roofer had carefully slid a new beam in place to shore up the damaged beam and the trough was sealed once more, our budget for the summer had taken a hard hit.

*   *   *

I would not have believed that there was a social life at '*la déchetterie*'. That's the French word for the garbage dump. Furthermore, I had no idea why the word used the feminine adjective *la*. But that aside, there was something to be learned here about life in our village. I had a mountain of small branches and twigs to dispose of after I had cut down the oak tree in the garden. So I began piling the debris onto a tarpaulin, tying it up and stuffing it, along with the broken tiles, into the hatchback of our car. This meant a number of trips, but fortunately the dump was nearby.

I had dropped off refuse there once before. That time, the man in charge had asked me where I lived. It seemed like an odd question, but I had told him Serre de Reynier in Nyons and pointed up the hill toward our house. He didn't say anything more and just walked back to his chair by the shed. I learned later that if I had been from outside Nyons, he would have told me that I couldn't drop off the refuse and would have sent me packing.

This time, when I drove up the ramp beside the bins with the first load of tree branches, I had barely unlatched the hatchback when the caretaker appeared beside me looking at the contents of the tarpaulin and the broken roof tiles.

"*Ah, là, le ratissage . . . et là, le béton . . .,*" he said, jabbing his finger toward one bin and then another.

The dump was a compound behind a high wire fence with gates that were locked after hours—not so much to prevent theft as it was unlikely anyone would want to steal junk, but to stop people from leaving trash that didn't belong there or might be placed in a wrong bin. There were five bins in all, each huge and at least eight feet deep. A ramp had been built alongside so that cars and trucks could easily drive up and unload. There were two men in charge to make sure that everyone used the right bins.

The hours were strict. It was open from eight in the morning until noon and did not reopen again until two. I learned that one day when I drove through the gates a few minutes before noon and one of the caretakers began advancing aggressively toward my car, waving me off.

"*Non, non!*" he said, and then other words that I didn't understand, all the while gesticulating energetically. It was clear he didn't want me there.

41

"*Pourquoi*—why?"

He tapped at his watch and began to move his hands back and forth with the palms facing down. That meant no. I glanced at my watch. It was five to twelve. I had five minutes. However, the unwritten French law of 'never work at lunch' had already kicked in.

"*Un petit moment*—that's all," I said.

He hesitated just a moment too long, leaving me an opening that I took, and I drove up the ramp. It required only a minute to empty the tarpaulin of twigs into the appropriate bin and drive down the ramp, but he was already standing at the gate waiting to lock it behind me. I smiled my best smile and waved.

Over time, I kept running into people I knew and at first thought it was just one of those coincidences. But gradually, I became aware that there was also an active social life at *la déchetterie*. One day François was unloading hedge trimmings from his truck. We warmly greeted each other and passed a few words before getting on with unloading our vehicles. Another time I met our plumber, and we shook hands and chatted. Then I noticed that others were doing the same thing. Sometimes the ramp was crowded with vehicles while the drivers stood talking amiably, waiting their turn. If unloading junk was a slow process, it was even slower the moment two acquaintances showed up, for all the correct social etiquette had to be followed: the greeting, shaking of hands and some polite discussion that inevitably led to other subjects.

Once I saw a woman drive in and pull up to the back of the line. The men promptly stopped their conversation, helped her unload her vehicle and sent her on her way. This was clearly a man's hang-out, and I slowly realized that most of these people had either a passing acquaintance with each other, or were friends, or even relatives. This was part of village life, and sooner or later everyone met here.

On another day I saw the older of the two caretakers yelling at a man who had just dropped an old bike into one of the bins. I watched as the man sheepishly crawled over the edge of the bin and down inside it. The caretaker now pointed at another bin and continued to yell at the man who climbed out and carried his bit of junk over to the correct bin.

"By now you must know that the caretaker is 'the colonel of the dump'," Hélène said when I told her what had occurred. "He's the one in charge and he takes his work totally seriously. That's his turf—and don't mess with him!"

Chapter 6
how to behave in haute société

We had received an invitation for dinner at the home
of our *notaire, Maître* Gérard Grandclès. This was unexpected and carried the implication that 'society' in Nyons
was prepared to have a look at us. Or, maybe we had more
Canadian friends who would like to buy property in France.
Whatever the case, we were delighted and quickly accepted.
A '*maître*' is a person who is considered a master of his discipline, a person of authority in his professional field. We
met him as the notary public who handled the purchase
of our house, and I recalled how the seller had deferred
to him. *Maître* Grandclès had been aloof and professional
that day.

In the brief phone conversation my wife had with
him, there was no specific time mentioned, and she had
been sufficiently surprised that she hadn't thought to ask.
Rather than phone him back, we decided to dress in smart

summer clothing and simply present ourselves at 7:30 on the appointed evening.

It turned out that the home of the *maître* and his wife was in the middle of a vineyard a few kilometres from Nyons. As we turned off the highway and drove up the single lane of a gravel road, a tall hedge of cypress trees formed a solid wall on the north side of the property. The road led to one end of this hedge where two massive stone pillars supported a great iron gate already open. Once inside, a tree-lined avenue led us to the house.

It was a classic two-storey stone farmhouse, or French *mas*. The gravel driveway opened into a wide area for parking and, as I pulled to a stop, I took in the vast green lawn, fruit and olive trees and the glitter of water that could only be a swimming pool. We got out of our car and walked, across gravel that crunched underfoot, toward a BMW M6 convertible parked near the front door.

"Are you sure this is the right day?" I asked, almost to myself.

"Why?"

"There aren't any other cars here."

"Oh, well, there's one. The *maître* drives an old Peugeot, so that BMW can't be his."

"But it *is*!" a man's voice said.

Maître Granclès came around the corner from the garden with his arms full of cut wood. He had a wide grin on his face as he walked over and put the wood down to greet us.

"Please, my hands are dirty." He offered his right wrist for me to shake and then leaned toward Hélène and proffered several air kisses, first to one cheek and then the other, all the while keeping his arms wide apart so as not to touch her white blouse. "Now, you have to call me Gerry, and my wife, who you will meet in a moment, is Lucienne or Lucie. By the way, I never take the BMW to work. My clients wouldn't approve."

He was behaving in a manner very different from that of the curt professional we had met at his office two years earlier. As he turned and walked toward the front door, I realized he was wearing old sandals, a stained T-shirt and shorts. He led us straight into a large open kitchen with a granite work station in the middle, above which hung pots and pans and every imaginable kitchen tool.

"*Chérie*," he announced loudly, "*les* Bitneys are *here*."

A woman came around the island with an even warmer smile than Gerry's, walked straight over to Hélène, hugged her and offered several welcoming words before turning to me to blow kisses past my cheeks.

Before we could muster anything to say, Gerry was heading out the door again. "I'll be back in a minute to mix drinks. I just have to set up the barbeque." And he was gone.

Without missing a beat, Lucie took over. "I've been waiting to meet you ever since Gerry told me about your move here. Hélène, do you like cooking? I adore it. Come over here and I'll show you what we're doing tonight. Gordon, would you lift down some martini glasses from the shelf over there?"

And with that, we were all drawn together into some part of the kitchen activity. Lucie had what looked like the largest whole rock cod I had ever seen on a wood cutting board before her and was vigorously scraping it in a very confident, hands-on manner. Then she picked it up in both hands and rolled it under the tap in the sink, rinsing away the loose scales. Next she flopped it back on the cutting board, took a large kitchen knife, held it in her hand with her index finger on one side of the blade and her thumb on the other and then quickly cut four bold diagonal slashes along one side of the fish before flipping it over and repeating the cuts on the other side. Her work was deft, not fussy, and all this was carried out while maintaining a running conversation with us.

Lucie lifted up the fish one last time and deposited it in a large pan. Next, she reached for a bowl containing a mixture of herb sprigs and began stuffing the cavity until the fish ballooned with protruding greenery. Then she poured generous amounts of olive oil over it and pulled two bowls to within easy reach. From the first, she took several tomatoes and, one by one, squeezed them in her fist, so that the red pulp and juice spilled out between her fingers and onto the fish. From the other, she took a handful of chopped herbs and rubbed them all over the fish until it glistened with a rainbow of colours. Pushing the pan with the fish to the side, her hands now shone with the same colours, so she turned to wash them in the sink. "There, that can marinate for a while."

"We like our martinis *le* James Bond style, shaken, not stirred, and with olives," Gerry said as he walked back in. "How about you? Or do you prefer wine? *J'ai des* single malt scotches." He was mixing French and English together with considerable ease.

Neither my wife nor I spoke up fast enough, so he did. "Martinis then!" He pulled a bottle of Tanqueray gin and another of vermouth from a cupboard. "We marinate *picholine* olives from our own trees just for martinis. Gordon, will you get some ice from the fridge?" He was already handing me an ice bucket.

As his wife had done with the fish, he made the martinis with a quick confidence, mixing the gin and vermouth unmeasured into the shaker along with some ice and then shaking it all in a chatter of noise. With all four glasses lined up in a row, he poured, dropped in the olives, and handed a glass to each of us.

"*Santé*," Lucie said, lifting her glass.

In a moment of silence, we all tasted the martinis.

"A martini should be like a cold cloud on the palate. It has to be made bone dry, so that it's crisp and subtle. The olive at the end is both the climax and the lure to have a second one. But I rarely do unless it's been a very bad day at the office. All that alcohol sneaks up on me like a cat that suddenly pounces." He winked.

We all laughed, and Lucie said, "Let's show you around before the others arrive."

For a *mas* that was hundreds of years old, the interior was remarkably modern. The kitchen had every convenience, including an aqua-coloured stove that stretched along one wall. The dining room opened through sliding glass doors to the garden and was furnished with an entire wall of glass cabinets. The massive glass table, already set for eight, rested on a stainless steel base, and the chairs were metal and leather. The living room could have been a showroom for Roche Bobois and also faced onto the garden and the swimming pool. By now it had become obvious to me that we had arrived before the accepted hour by Provence time and that the other guests were unlikely to appear for a while. First Gerry slipped away to change while Lucie kept us occupied, and then Lucie did the same, eventually returning in heels, linen pants and a fine silk blouse.

And then finally the doorbell rang and two other couples arrived.

Gerry popped champagne corks and began pouring. "Let's go out by the pool for a sip." And with that he led us out one of the sliding glass doors and into the garden.

As we walked across the lawn toward the swimming pool, the view opened to reveal a broad vista of the valley below checkered with vineyards and orchards and then beyond to an unimpeded view of Mont Ventoux in the distance.

We stood on the paving stones at the edge of the swimming pool, chatting and sipping the champagne while getting to know each other. Céline was a wine and food writer who was just finishing her latest book on the history of food (Gerry warned that we would hear about that), and her husband Émile was wealthy enough to be 'successfully unemployed.' As for the other couple, Colette was a journalist, and Guy gave wine lectures at l'Université du Vin at Suze-la-Rousse. Hélène described our backgrounds and what had brought us to Provence while Gerry circulated, topping up everyone's champagne glasses. And then Lucie called us to return indoors to the dining room. With the martini and then the champagne, my French had improved and my conversation was flowing with remarkable ease.

Once seated at the table, Guy turned to Émile and Céline. "Did you know that the idea for the modern French wine classification system, the *Appellation d'Origine Contrôlée* system or AOC, originated in Rome?" He paused a moment for emphasis. "It's true. The Romans created a pricing for an amphora of wine based on where the wine came from and its vintage. It was a sort of 'birth certificate' that was written on each amphora."

"I can tell you've been reading Brillat-Savarin, Guy," Céline smiled.

"Only to keep up with you, Céline."

"*Ha*, they're at it again," Colette quipped, glancing at Émile.

The conversation was flowing in waves now, moving from one end of the table to the other. Clearly, the people here knew each other well. Everyone seemed to have something different to say, as if seeking out a subject or direction for the conversation. And then I began to realize I was in the middle of a real contest of some sort. The combatants knew what they were about, and I was about to learn.

"Do you know that women are far more inclined to take pleasure in tasting a wine, while men analyse it?" Colette said. "But it's quite the reverse in marital relations—men think only about pleasure, while women look for pedigree."

"Thank you, dear!" Guy puffed up his chest in mock appreciation.

Céline ignored him and was already saying, "Did you know that bees have a sense of smell? That's what attracts them to flowers—the stronger the fragrance, the stronger the attraction. Men are like that, except in the case of bees the males are lazy drones."

"What else do flowers produce?" Émile asked, directing the conversation away from Céline and Guy.

"Perfume," someone said.

"Honey," Gerry added. "Did you know that Alexander the Great was embalmed in honey?"

"Do you know what 'sugaring off' is?" Hélène asked. There was a moment of silence. "It's the spring harvest of maple sugar in Quebec."

"What is the most expensive eatable in the world?" This came from Gerry as he rose to get something from the kitchen.

"*Truffes*," Colette said all too quickly.

"No!" Gerry hollered from the kitchen.

"Maybe caviar," Céline offered.

"No," Gerry said re-entering the room.

"Is it a liquid, or an herb or a spice?" Guy asked.

"Possibly," Gerry said, maintaining a blank face.

"Then it is Château d'Yquem."

"Nope." By this time Gerry was smiling. "It takes 4,000 to make thirty grams."

There was silence, so he went on. "Those thirty grams will cost one hundred *euros*."

As there was still no response, Gerry gave another hint. "Each flower only has three stamens."

"Of course—saffron—how stupid of me," Céline said.

The question-and-answer game had now run its course, and the focus shifted to a series of chats between parties seated next to each other.

Gerry and Lucie were kept busy between the dining room and the kitchen, always careful that one was at the table while the other was off tending to something. I could hear the fish sizzling on the barbeque. When Gerry had finished the grilling, Lucie carried it in like a trophy on a huge platter, sear marks from the metal fish basket branded into its sides. The tail and head were still attached and the look in its upturned eye spoke of wonder at what had happened to it.

Once again, Lucie worked with the same panache she had displayed in the kitchen. It occurred to me that this was a show they'd had plenty of experience with. She left the seared skin intact as she used two utensils to separate and lift the flesh away from the bones, placing each piece on plates that were then passed down the table. When one side of the fish had been served, she took hold of the tail and deftly lifted the entire bone structure along with the head away in one piece. With the other side of the fish now exposed, she continued serving. It was a masterpiece of presentation.

The conversation hadn't stopped as the plates moved around the table, for Colette was saying, "A gourmet enjoys tasting fine foods whereas a gourmand enjoys eating. So how do you distinguish a gourmet from a gourmand?"

"Belt size," Émile offered.

"One enjoys tasting, the other satisfaction," added Guy.

"And what distinguishes the two from an epicure?" she now asked.

"Pride," Lucie said, looking up from her work.

"Good!" Guy pronounced. "It's about ego."

"Can a gourmand be an epicure?" Colette went on.

"Sure, but the Englishman Glenway Wescott summed up a gourmand this way—'You could see the gourmandise shining on his rosy lips.'"

"Yuck," muttered Colette wrinkling her nose in disgust. "That's sort of the opposite of an epicure."

"I get tired of people lauding the cork," Guy said. "It's a throwback to another age, an historical anachronism that won't die because it's entrenched in the ritual of enjoying wine. Corks only came into use in the 17th century. Before that, the necks of wine bottles were stuffed with oily rags. You can imagine how successful that was and why the cork was a quantum leap forward at the time. It sealed the bottle, was largely neutral to the wine and permitted easy shipping and storage. But it also has a failure rate. Gerry, how many well-aged bottles have you opened and found the wine corked?"

"Too often, maybe one bottle in twenty or thirty."

"Yes, and you paid for that wine. We all know a bad cork can taint the wine and ruin it—that wet dog smell. Some people argue it lets the wine breathe—sure, all the way through that metal cap that's then put on top. There's a lot of mythology going on here—the romance of the cork and corkscrew, the ritual of slowly opening a bottle that's been laid away for ten or twenty years, the anticipation of the experience. Would you enjoy your Château Lafite as much if it had a screw top rather than a cork? Not likely. But do you mind losing one bottle to a bad cork in every few cases? There've been studies done comparing natural corks to things like artificial corks and screw tops. Do you know what's the best stopper? It's a common pop bottle cap."

"But can you imagine the aura, the mystique, around popping the cap off your five- or six-hundred-*euro* bottle of Lafite like a Pepsi?" Colette said, laughingly.

"Well, it may be that wines made for quick profit and quick drinking should have a bottle cap," Émile said. "But, you can't reseal a bottle with just a cap."

"So it's the screw top then," Gerry said rather conclusively.

Céline turned to look at me. "So tell me, Gordon, why did you and Hélène buy a home here?"

The directness of the question caught me off guard. "Well . . ." I ventured, gathering my thoughts. "The climate is certainly one factor. But I enjoy wine, the Roman history, beautiful medieval villages and the French lifestyle. Then there are the places where artists like Cézanne and Van Gogh painted, and *ferias* for the bullfights that Picasso attended. We've seen some of them and—"

"You're still thinking like a visitor here," Céline said, cutting me off. "But that's all right, for you are trying to find your Provence and no doubt you will." Then, as unexpectedly as she had tackled me, she turned to the others around the table. "What do you think is the perfect complement to a dish?"

As if on cue, suggestions flowed from around the table to change the subject. Was it pine nuts with fresh green beans? Or pesto with salmon? Butter dripping off green asparagus held between your fingers? Truffles with eggs? Champagne with caviar?

"So what is it?" Hélène finally asked.

"In fact, it's something far more mundane," Céline went on, "so much so that it is generally overlooked. It is from the New World and took Europe by storm. It offers nothing of remarkable culinary character. It doesn't titillate the taste buds or create a stir. It just took its place quietly and has remained a staple in dining that goes unnoticed."

"Come on, Céline!" Guy pressed.

"It is just the potato," Céline announced. "It's so integrated into our cuisine we forget to notice it. How often do you see meat served without it? And if you have, did it taste right or did the entire dish seem somehow a bit off balance and in need of something else? We tend to dwell on the spectacular flavours and miss the rudimentary ones that show them off. Potatoes can be prepared in all sorts of ways— baked, boiled and mashed or puréed, *au gratin*, pan-fried, deep-fried and more. They have the ability to complement almost any dish—take the strong flavour of meats that are even better when put opposite the potato's unassuming flavour. It has created wholly new food combinations such as fish and chips."

"Talking about carbohydrates, what shape and colour is *figatelli?*" Guy aimed the question at Céline.

"Spiral and brown," she ventured all too cautiously.

"*Hah!* It isn't a pasta. *Figatelli* is a Corsican sausage made principally from pork liver and usually highly spiced with salt, pepper and garlic," he said in triumph.

Somehow I knew this sort of conversation had been played out on other nights.

"Céline," Colette interjected, "I still remember last spring when you convinced those two poor women that Alfredo Fettucini was an Italian hair stylist who tied ribbons in ladies' hair."

"Yes, that was fun."

Colette was seated next to me, and on seeing me sniffing the wine in my glass opted out of the banter and turned to me. "The whites in Provence aren't the best in the world. The reds can be a lot more rewarding. They can be massive and full of the wild *terroir* here. I understand in North America you have a slightly gamey wine called Zinfandel. Is that so?"

I told her what I knew about Zinfandel—its elasticity as a grape, able to make wines as light as strawberries or as rich as a port.

"What is a Shiraz? We don't see that wine here. I am told it is the Mae West of wine. Wasn't she the sexy Hollywood actress?"

"Shiraz is the Australian name for Syrah. It's—"

"I've read that it's a big, fleshy, full-bodied style," Guy interjected. Fresh from his victory with Céline, he must have noticed me ducking the Mae West comparison. "It's our Syrah grape, but with the accent that down-unders carry about on their tongues it comes out as 'shee-raahz'. Now, since our play is with foods tonight, let's talk about the time-honoured institution of restaurants. They've been around since man began selling food."

"But they haven't!" Céline cut in, taking up the challenge. "At least, not by our definition of a restaurant. Not one existed before the 1760s. They came out of a loophole in the guild system. In fact, it was a royal prerogative granted by the king."

Guy began grinning like a Cheshire cat that had spotted a mouse walking into its trap. Untroubled, Céline went straight on. There was something in her confident manner that made me wonder what she had in mind.

"They're an invention of the 18th century," she said. "Before that, there were just places like inns and taverns with *table d'hôtes* that offered only the most basic of food that the diners shared at a common table. The guilds regulated all trade and eating places. Then, in the 1760s, Roze de Chantoiseau purchased a royal privilege to operate a place that offered broths as medicinal restoratives. These were thought to cure ailments and restore health. The places that sold these restoratives became known as '*restaurants*'.

"Since restoratives were considered medicinal rather than food, and since they existed by royal privilege and were outside the guild rules, they could fix their own hours and offer a private table rather than that common table of a *table d'hôte*. Here's a curious little tidbit—the broth was squirted into the diner's bowl with a large syringe, and if the diner didn't promptly pay for it, the restaurateur would take it back using the same syringe.

"At first these restaurants sold just broths, but gradually, with their royal prerogative in hand, they began offering solid foods. Then they came up with their greatest idea—a printed *carte*, or menu, providing a choice of foods at fixed prices. For the first time, a diner could chose from a list what he wanted to eat and at a price he could afford. By contrast, the '*table d'hôtes*' were restricted by guild rules to serve only at specified times a fixed common meal with no menu, for which diners paid 'by head'. Restaurants had a distinct competitive advantage over the inns and taverns. Common tables were rough-and-ready places to dine. The ability to dine at private tables and private rooms had its advantages. Moreover, women were now able to dine out in the more civilized surroundings with companions of their choice."

Guy looked up from his plate with a look of defeat. "Bested on the turn of a word."

The timing was perfect, for Lucie brought in dessert, and Gerry strode back into the room with a sparkle in his eyes and two bottles wrapped in brown paper that he was waving in the air to show off.

"What's this—a blind tasting?" Hélène said.

"Yes," he said as he uncorked the bottles and began pouring the wines into fresh glasses. "I have two wines for you to taste. They are unblended varietals. Tell me what you think of them."

I sniffed the first glass of wine and then tasted the contents. It was a gloriously heady Roussanne with a scent that almost leaped from the glass; certainly not the beguilingly fine and aromatic wine from farther north but an in-your-face, full-bodied Roussanne that was unctuous

57

on the palate, rich beyond belief with hints of almonds and wild flowers and other things that were harder to identify.

I tried the second wine and was hit immediately with the characteristics of marzipan, so it had to be a Marsanne. It was so rich it could have been a dessert wine. Everyone was silent, nosing and sipping the wines.

"*Ça, ce sont les soeurs, l'une et l'autre,*" Émile said. "They're like sisters raised in the same house, but they have very different personalities. Where did you find them?"

"They are made by a Danish couple who have a vineyard in Condorcet, just a few hills east of Nyons. I don't know of any other wines that are quite the same as these."

We all continued tasting, as both wines were complex and took time to explore. Then Gerry rose abruptly from the table.

"*Et maintenant pour des* single-malt scotch. I have a great selection. *Très magnifique,*" he added, waving for everyone to follow him into the living room.

Chapter 7
le temps des cerises & scented blue hills

As THE DAYS FLOWED BY our old habits of self-imposed schedules, deadlines and planned activities slowly lost importance. A new rhythm took its place: biking early each morning for the paper and croissants and then a more serious ride later; my wife's running routine; the Thursday market in our village; pruning the shrubs and hedges and the things we kept finding that needed attention. Without self-imposed schedules, each day and week lost any special meaning and they flowed together, one just following the other.

I had begun riding for the exercise but then discovered that there was an explorer in me who wanted to get to know the surrounding countryside. So my longer rides became small expeditions as I searched out more challenging back roads leading to places farther afield. I began to plan each ride in advance with one or another of the maps I had purchased, continually seeking new terrain. I was getting to know the nearby villages like Valréas and Grignan as I pedalled through their narrow streets before heading off once more along the country roads. One day, in a limitless blue sky, armadas of white clouds were sailing by. Like a racer with a challenge, I tried to stay with them, but no matter how hard I pedalled they moved on, leaving me far behind.

As the weather improved, I wore just a pair of shorts, runners and an old loose T-shirt. All the same, I had learned to tuck a light nylon shell into a sack in case the weather changed. My only concessions to proper cycling gear were riding gloves and a helmet. I didn't have the stylish clothing I saw all the French riders invariably wearing. Then one day I nodded at a French rider wearing a stunning outfit. He glanced at my clothes and smiled wryly as he rode on by.

The next day I dropped into a *magasin de vélo*. The salesman looked me over with the quick eye of an experienced *haute couturier* sizing up a good sale. He showed me several vibrantly coloured outfits, all made of stretchy, body-clinging Lycra that displayed every bone and muscle, or lack thereof. Clearly these were made for well-toned athletes. I explained that I just wanted something simple, definitely not extravagantly expensive, that did not have to come with an Hermès label as I was not going to be seen on the Champs-Elysées riding alongside Lance Armstrong at the end of the Tour de France. I managed to find an outfit that was not too flashy, suited my purposes and that, to my satisfaction, the salesman thoroughly disapproved of. Having lost that sales effort, he redirected his energies to finding a colour-coordinated helmet, gloves and proper shoes. "*C'est nécessaire!*" He kept saying, raising his voice a bit more each time he met with my resistance. Finally, having glanced at my all-purpose bike with something like scorn, he restrained himself to recommending the proper shoes.

The transaction completed and my image remade, I knew that I would look a bit less out of place in a sport that I was learning had to be done *de rigueur*. All I had to do was get over feeling that I had just bought a skintight Spiderman costume I would actually be wearing in full public view the next day.

•   •   •

There are customs that vary from one culture to another. Often these are subtle and difficult to observe and then adapt to. The greeting kiss as practiced in France is a good example. The way it works is that on meeting, kisses are exchanged on each others' cheeks. This is meant to be a quick, graceful set of movements: a little peck here and a little peck there, choreographed and timed to perfection—a little minuet, honed from a lifetime of experience. However, bring a stranger to this custom and it quickly changes into an uncertain and even risky challenge, causing even those well-experienced to suddenly become nervous and hesitant. You may ask: What could be so complicated about a simple kiss on the cheek . . . ? Simple, that is, until I tried it. It is called *le bisou*.

First of all, *le bisou* has levels of subtle meaning that accompany it. What was the correct number of kisses? Anywhere from one to four, it turns out. Where were they to be directed? And where did the hands belong? Eye contact seemed to be important as well, part of the recognition, and it had to take place along with an appropriate word or two just before *le bisou*.

61

So how did the novice start? My attempts were a case in point. Simply observing would not do, for what was expected in one situation might not be the same for the next. When meeting a lady for the first time, *le bisou* might not even be appropriate, although it was more than likely correct for a second meeting. All the same, the practice varied enough to keep me hanging at bay, hesitantly watching for some sign as to what to do. If the lady leaned slightly forward while shaking hands with me, I felt I was on safe ground to lean forward as well. But then there was the question of which cheek to kiss, right or left. To complicate things more, apparently the practice varies depending on where one is in France. If my readers are confused by now, it is not surprising because I certainly was.

So I consulted the best mind on the subject—my wife.

"Good question," she said replied, obviously flattering me in order to relax my knit eyebrows.

"One kiss is considered polite and formal. It's proper courtesy with a stranger. The kiss is to the left cheek, in other words you move to the right. But your lips never actually touch the cheek, and above all do not make a kissing noise with the lips—that's gauche. Two kisses, one on each cheek means a warm greeting with someone you already know. But if you know the person very well, then three *bisous* may be in order. You'll know because the woman will offer up her cheek one more time and all you have to do is comply. The max is four kisses, and that's only for relations and the very closest of friends, so I hope you'll never get to that one."

My ear picked up a subtle statement there.

Having taken all that in, I thought I had it down and could now pull it off suavely and with style. The perfect opportunity arose when, soon after, our neighbours introduced us to another couple. I leaned forward and to the left, only to suddenly realize I'd mixed up right and left, and my lips were headed for the wrong cheek. *Madame* tried to correct my error by offering up the other cheek in mid-forward movement just as I recognized my error. The result was a dance of errors until neither of us could escape the inevitable, and I planted a kiss squarely on her nose. It was far too late to do anything more than for us both to pull back and move on. It was at that moment I realized out of the corner of my eye that others in the room had observed the blunder—and were no doubt writing me off as an oaf they had mistakenly welcomed into their midst.

It was still May, and the *brulat* variety of cherries on our tree wouldn't be ready for picking for another month. However, other varieties had shown up in the market already. There is something about cherries that no other fruit quite matches: blood-red, luscious fruit the colour of a beating heart, and plump, taut skin. The French have a song, *Le temps des cerises*, extolling the joy of cherries in the spring when the heart is open to love.

Riding the back roads one morning I spotted men in an orchard picking cherries while balancing at the top of ladders. I glided to a stop and watched. "Can I buy some?" I asked one the workers.

He gave me a Gallic shrug and directed me to an elderly woman standing nearby, so I repeated my question to her.

"*Mais oui!*" she said so enthusiastically, I could almost see her mind converting her cherries into coins.

"*Combien?*" I asked, wanting to know the price before I committed.

"*Dix le kilo.*"

I hesitated, thinking ten *euros* for a kilo of cherries was far too expensive. Then I realized she probably still thought in the old currency of French *francs*. After all, the stores still priced their goods in both *francs* and *euros*, even though *francs* were no longer legal tender and had no value.

"*Et en euros?*" I asked in a soft voice.

"*Deux*"—two, she said awkwardly, hardly glancing at me.

I bought more than I needed and rode home with a full basket on my bike.

Hélène picked one out of the bag and bit into it, then wrinkled her nose.

"These are sour cherries. I'll make a *clafoutis* if you'll do the pitting and buy some *crème fraîche*."

Nothing more had to be said—a quick ride and I returned with *crème fraîche*.

With the arrival of summer solstice, poppies appeared, spattering the rocky hillsides and wild meadows with dashes of red. Hélène had me stop the car at one field so she could pick a handful that were still budding and unopened. Once home, she put them in an old vase of rough pottery with their wiry stems aiming the reddening buds in every direction.

By the beginning of July poppies had been replaced by blue lavender, and as I cycled the back roads, I came to know all the fields on our hilltop and their invisible clouds of fragrance. Lavender was once hand-cut with sickles by women wearing skirts that hung to the ground and then taken by horse-drawn carts to the village to be distilled into an intense, heady essence. Today, mechanical harvesting and trucks have eliminated that hard labour, but the distillation process remains basically unchanged. One day, I stopped at the distillery and watched the men unloading truckloads of lavender and filling the empty still. Later, I could see a wisp of blue-grey smoke rising and forming a faint haze over Nyons, held there by the surrounding hills. The scent remained in the air throughout the long harvest.

As I rolled into the driveway after one of my rides, Hélène was kneeling on the gravel patio, wiping something down with a rag.

"Hi," was all I said as I wheeled over and leaned my bike against the house. I told her about the lavender.

"Yes. It's as if someone tossed swathes of blue corduroy in the fields. I drove through a cloud of perfume the other day. But look at what I've found!"

I stepped closer and took in what appeared to be a twisted piece of rusty wrought-iron.

"It's an old wrought-iron table frame."

There must have had a sceptical look on my face, for she added, "Well, yes, it has no top. With a little paint and a new top it'll make a great coffee table. One curved leg was sticking out of the metal bin at *la déchetterie*. So I reached in and tried pulling it out. The 'colonel' immediately came over and told me to leave it there. My *gawd*, you wouldn't believe the struggle I had appealing to his gallant side. Then he relented and helped me pull it out of the bin. We looked it over, and it was so nicely designed that I asked him if I could have it. At first he said it wasn't possible—'*c'est pas possible*' he said, about as stiffly as he could manage. He must have

65

seen my disappointment, for he finally gave in and actually put it in the back of my car—but not before saying that I mustn't tell anyone that he let me have 'state property'. I'll take him some cherries from our tree to thank him. And will you make a tile top for the table? I know just the tiles."

.   .   .

The French have managed to acquire a reputation for remaining slim and having an unusually low incidence of heart attacks. On the other hand, they are also renowned for their gastronomic ways. That apparent contradiction has drawn a lot of attention from people in other countries. Foreigners have even put a name to it—the French Paradox. Some suggest it is the use of olive oil instead of butter in the diet, but that doesn't account for the northern areas where butter remains on most tables. All sorts of theories have been put forward and even studies done in attempts to find an answer. After all, who wouldn't like a way to eat well and remain slim at the same time? Researchers have offered sophisticated ideas like higher rates of metabolism and a less indolent way of life. Whatever the reason, the issue has remained unsolved. However, my wife had become interested. She noticed that many women remained unusually slim. In fact, some of the women in Nyons were so slim "they would pass for anorexic", she exclaimed.

"How do they do it?" she asked out loud one day, not really addressing the question to me. I could tell that she was about to set off to find an answer.

We had been invited to sumptuous dinners in French homes with multiple courses of rich food and different wines poured with every course. We saw men eat lunches out accompanied by half a carafe of wine followed by dessert. We even began to believe that the French Paradox might have some validity to it, and if we could only find out what it was, we too could drink wine and dine without concern about gaining unwanted pounds.

Hélène began by asking the women she knew, but no one seemed to understand a question like 'Why are you so slim?' or 'What do you do for exercise?' It was clear that the women of Provence didn't exercise like North American women. In fact, they didn't exercise at all, from what Hélène could see. There were a few gyms, and they were used almost exclusively by men. She had dropped into the one in Nyons, named Iles Verte (no doubt named to conjure up an image of paradise) and returned home to report that the men smoked cigarettes between sets of weightlifting. They expressed surprise to see her there.

The pharmacies offered their own remedy. I would look in their display windows when passing to see large posters displaying products for weight loss. These ads invariably showed the perfectly proportioned legs of some fabulously beautiful woman that were fully exposed as she applied a cream with one hand while holding its tube in the other, so that the label could be easily read by anyone walking by. The statement on the posters boldly extolled the powers of losing weight simply by regular applications of the cream to her legs.

"Do the women here really think they can lose weight that way?" I asked my wife, almost in a whisper, as I looked at the poster.

"Sure they do. Besides, it doesn't matter whether it works or not. The fact is, the people who use it believe it does and they feel better for it."

"But could it *really* work?"

"Of course not. You have to remember the women here don't exercise. *We* go to the gym and work out; *they* use creams."

Each time I walked by the village pharmacy I looked at the poster. Clearly, it sold lots of cream.

We began to watch and think about the meals we saw people eating. Yes, there were huge portions offered at lunch, and yes the diners certainly ordered and ate all the food. Yet we also knew that the typical continental breakfast consisted of some bread and possibly cold cuts and not much more, just the opposite of an English—or worse, an Irish—breakfast. And then some things began to fall into place. . . . We were seeing people eating only in circumstances where they were enjoying food. The French kitchens we saw were invariably as small as a broom closet and certainly not a place to gather. Lunch out was an event. Weekends were for celebratory dining, the enjoyment of wine and good food.

Then one day, Hélène decided to have lunch with our realtor, a woman she referred to as 'model thin'. Her plan was to slide in the question during lunch and find out for herself. As should have been expected, the woman almost asked what the word 'diet' meant.

"These women just don't eat the way they talk," she said when she returned after lunch. "The word 'diet' exists in the French language—it's *le régime*. Yet that woman won't own up to dieting even though her ribs almost pierce her skin. I watched her. She ordered a salad, pushed it around on her plate, ate a bit, didn't touch the fresh *baguette* and drank just mineral water, no wine. Some paradox. It's all about starvation!"

I had spent most of my life in Western Canada and was realizing that I was somewhat at sea in France, where I was struggling with the language and the cultural differences. I felt ungrounded. So I began haunting the village librairie and buying books on the history and way of life in Provence. Surely, I thought, understanding its history would give me a better footing. Often Hélène would find me reading and working at my computer.

"You're a workaholic. When are you going to start to slow down?"

"Soon, I hope."

One morning I noticed something on the floor next to the leg of the desk. It looked like dust. Not thinking much about it, I got out the broom and a dustpan, swept it up and continued with what I was doing. A few days later I noticed that more dust had accumulated in the same spot. I knelt down to take a closer look and realized that there was more than one pile, and when I rubbed some between my fingers, it even felt like sawdust. Next, I looked up at the underside of the desk. I could just make out some small holes in the wood above the first pile. In fact, there were similar small holes above the other piles. There was only one conclusion—the desk had wood-boring insects. The only place I had seen anything like this was in very expensive antique furniture stores, where the dealer proudly showed off the holes as proof of the age and authenticity of the piece he was trying to sell. I had also heard that an electric drill worked almost as well.

Not knowing what to do, I just swept up the piles now and then. However, this was not a solution, for the bugs could easily and all too contentedly move on to other pieces of furniture. I wondered: If I put my ear to the desk would I hear a gnawing sound? Something had to be done. The next Friday François arrived, and when we stopped work in the garden for coffee, I raised the subject.

"*Pas de problème*," he said, showing immediate understanding.

"*Utilisez une seringue de poison.*"

"*Une ser-ang?*" I repeated, trying to grasp the word, half thinking that if I sounded it out I could guess its meaning.

"*Oui, une ser-in-gue,*" he repeated, slowly pronouncing every syllable while pushing his thumb between his next two fingers.

"Ah—a syringe!" I said catching on. "But where can I get a *ser-in-gue?*"

"*À la pharmacie dans le village.*"

"*Et le poison?*"

He promised to bring some poison the next Friday. Coffee finished, we went back to work.

The following day I dropped into the pharmacy and was greeted by a smiling young woman who asked what she could do for me.

"*Je veux une seringue, si'l vous plaît,*" I said.

Her smile remained but took on a crinkled look, and I thought I saw her eyes narrow slightly as she inspected me. Why did I want a syringe, she asked.

"*J'ai quelques insectes dans le bois de mon secrétaire,*" I said, explaining that I had bugs in my desk.

She looked at me with what I thought was heightened curiosity. Clearly she did not see the connection between a syringe and insects. Then an old-fashioned camera bulb went off in my head, and I realized that a better explanation was needed.

"*J'injecte le poison dans les trous qu'ont fait les insectes,*" I said, making the same motion with my fingers as François had done, hoping she would understand my motion to represent injecting poison into the holes in the desk and not my arm.

"Ah," she nodded, not looking at all convinced. "*C'est tout?*"

Yes, that was all I wanted.

She went to the back of the pharmacy and returned moments later with a syringe sealed in a plastic wrapper. I paid for it, picked up the package from the countertop where it was lying and headed for the door. I could sense her concerned eyes on me as the door closed behind me.

When François arrived with the poison and I injected the holes in the desk. Over the ensuing weeks the small piles of sawdust did not reappear. For some time after that, I was happy not to return to the pharmacy. And when I occasionally had to walk by the window, I no longer glanced at the poster of the model with the perfect legs.

Chapter 8
how to dine on herbs and pastries and other things French

ALL IT TOOK WAS WORKING in our garden to discover the herbs growing wild in Provence. Hidden among the weeds I came upon tufts of thyme and scruffy bits of sage that, once liberated, thrived anew as if welcoming my attention. Whenever I rubbed against the new growth of rosemary in the driveway hedge, its resinous, almost camphor scent came away on my hand. I mistook a fledgling bay tree for an unwanted shrub and nearly cut it down.

We bought a range of potted herbs: several varieties of parsley, subtle oregano, chives, several mints and thirsty basil that demanded daily watering. These were set in a row on the balcony next to the kitchen, and whenever one was needed for a dish, we stepped out and clipped some. The bottles of dried herbs we had purchased at the Intermarché when we first arrived remained forgotten at the back of the kitchen cupboard.

Fresh herbs, so readily available, changed the way we dined. Now it was new potatoes boiled lightly and dressed with butter and freshly cut parsley; bruschetta on a slice of *baguette* using farm-ripened tomatoes, garlic and chopped basil, all drenched with our green Nyons olive oil and accompanied by a cool, tart white wine; a Dijon mustard coating with an abundance of garden sage for pork chops barbequed over coals from the oak tree I had cut down earlier; a small pizza with cheese and tomato slices spread like coins on top, lightly roasted and then garnished with basil leaves for their pungent scent of anise and clove.

Hélène also began to cook differently, not adding a lot of extra things to complicate the dish. "Let the ingredients speak for themselves. Keep it simple—don't disguise them behind a lot of other unnecessary flavours," she said.

When planning lunch or dinner we would often start by thinking about the herbs and after that decide what to prepare. The new spring growth of rosemary from the hedge led to a leg of lamb that Hélène butterflied and barbequed. It called for red wine, so I opened two bottles. One was made from Grenache grapes and the other Mouvèdre. The Grenache was round and soft with berries and young tannins but lacked something, while the other was all backbone—as hard as ink and unyielding. Neither tasted quite right. So I did the unthinkable and took out a third glass and began to blend the two wines, first equally, and then changing the proportions and tasting until I was satisfied that a mix of sixty per cent Grenache to forty per cent Mouvèdre was better.

Once, at the Thursday market, I bought a salmon mousse in the fish aisle and paired it with a bottle of Viognier from

73

Condrieu. The result was spectacular. The apricot peach nectar of the Viognier set against the richness of the mousse raised the experience to a whole new level that neither offered alone.

The French have a passion for freshly baked goods, beginning with the very famous and ubiquitous *baguette*—that two-foot-long, thin white bread with a toasted crust and a white inner core that melted in the mouth. It outsold all the other breads and was the one that workers carried home under their sweaty armpits. Listening to our neighbour Jean one evening as he talked about which bakeries he liked best, I realized that there are actually *baguette* connoisseurs. He could distinguish between the products of each *boulangerie* in Nyons and talked about ones from other villages nearby. On one occasion we had risen early to climb Montagne d'Angèle, and *en route* he stopped at a *boulangerie* in a village we were passing through. When he got back in the car with several fresh *baguettes* in his arms, he told us that he liked this particular baker's bread for the hints of hazelnut in the crust.

To shop for breads, I had to learn their names. It was embarrassing just pointing at loaves on the shelves in the *boulangeries* rather than asking for a bread by name. A *baguette* was easy, for everyone knew what that was, but what about all those other shapes and colours that sat out of reach behind the counter? So I found myself listening to the women's orders and matched the names to what the *boulanger* then reached for and wrapped in paper.

A *ficelle*, or string, is about the same length as a *baguette* but thinner with a crispier crust. A *flûte* is between those two in size. The baker might want to braid the bread or make a circle called a *couronne*—a wreath—or even cut notches along its length so that it resembled an ear of corn. Then there is *pain*—basically a fat *baguette*. A *bâtard* is a small pain, and a *fougasse* is a flattened *bâtard*. There is one shaped like a ball, so of course it was called a *boule* or *boulot*. A bun is a *petit pain*. It became clear that some breads are named by their shape, others by the flour used or by added things like figs or olives. At first I kept my orders simple and stayed with the names I knew. Then, slowly, as I learned the words I ventured to try other ones, arriving home with new shapes and crusts.

Bread must be freshly made each day, so in the very early hours of the morning the *boulanger* rolls the dough into *boules* or balls which he then shapes and bakes into *pains* or loaves. An inventive *boulanger* might choose to turn his occupation into an art form to show off just how good he is; hence displayed next to the more conventional shapes in his window there might be a crispy bike, a bridge or even a miniature version of the Eiffel Tower.

.   .   .

We had been eating fattening little butter-laced croissants while reading the *Trib* each morning. In fact, I had been buying croissants and *pain au chocolat* from all the *boulangeries* in Nyons to find out if there was really any discernible difference. Between us we were forming an opinion. It was coming down to a tie between Boulangerie de Barjavel and a place operated by two ladies on a corner of Place Colonel Barillon. The ladies probably had the edge as they offered two different croissants, one with a normal amount of butter and another with *double beurre*. Clearly there were plenty of people in Nyons who did not stick to a diet as the *double beurre* always sold out first. Furthermore, their pastry was lighter and flakier. Compared to day-old pastry on supermarket shelves that was soft and tough, these were exquisite things, just minutes from the oven, crisp and melting in the mouth.

I liked my croissants with tart jellies like quince or red currant, but far and away the best, when we had the chance to buy it, was the floral-scented rose petal jelly from Fauchon in Paris or Fortnum & Mason in London. Aside from being hard to find, these jellies were budget-busters and purchased as rare treats. Even though there is next to no nutritional value, croissants with jelly and a pot of coffee came close to an ethereal experience.

We did not realize it at first, however, we had also become addicted to the *Trib*. This became clear when one sunny morning I rode into the village for the usual purchases, stopped at the *tabac* for the newspaper and found that the stands normally crammed with newspapers were empty. I looked around to make sure, but there were no newspapers on the floor, the counter or anywhere in sight.

"*Pas de journal?*" I asked the woman behind the counter.

"*En grève*," she said tersely, and then added "*à Marseille*," with something close to contempt in her voice.

So there was a strike in Marseille. This was hardly a surprise, considering the pleasure the French derived from a good *grève*. But, all the same, it was about to leave an empty spot in the routine of our mornings.

I rode home, delivered this news, and we sat down, poured ourselves mugs of coffee and ate the fresh croissants. We made light conversation to fill the void created by the lack of reading material, but our conversation seemed forced without a headline to comment on or an article to take issue with. We finally gave up and rose from the table to wash up the dishes. Could a newspaper really be that important? The next day was no better. We were almost hunting for something to talk about. Part of our morning routine had gone missing. I don't think either of us had realized how important it was—all for want of a newspaper. By the third morning, the croissants were eaten, coffee sipped quickly and dishes cleared so that we could get on with our day.

Then, after five days of stopping at the *tabac* to find the stands empty, I was surprised to find them stocked with newspapers once again. The woman behind the counter was smiling.

Maybe the temporary loss of the newspaper, which upset our early morning routine, was what set off the ensuing event. In any event, my wife made an announcement. "I'm in France, and I'm going to make croissants," she said as she lowered her section of the newspaper.

"That's interesting," I replied. "It sounds like a wonderful idea. You can probably find the pastry at Intermarché in their frozen food section."

"Oh, no. I want to make them from scratch. That way I can learn what all is involved."

And with that the project started. First she researched the Internet for a good recipe. That was easy enough to find. All that was needed was flour, butter, yeast, eggs, milk, water, sugar and salt—and for *pain au chocolat*, some semi-sweet dark chocolate. Next came the clearing of the kitchen counters in preparation for the effort. This also meant the end to my buying croissants in the village every morning.

A YouTube site had a ten-minute video course that advised the home baker to allow a good half-day for preparation in order to make the less complicated version of croissants. The instructor also informed us that the word was pronounced *kwa'san* (with the 'r' and the 't' silent) and stemmed from both its crescent shape and the French verb *croisser*, meaning 'to grow' or 'puff up'. After watching the video several times, and with the ingredients purchased and spread out on the counter, Hélène set to work.

It looked easy enough: just prepare the dough, roll it with a rolling pin so that it is as thin as possible and apply a thin layer of butter. Then fold the dough with the butter inside, roll it out flat once more and repeat the process several more times. The dough and butter are layered at least nine times, and if you are a keen baker then keep doing this until there are more than thirty layers. Gently fold the dough one last time and place it in the refrigerator for a day to allow the yeast to work and the dough to rise. The following day, remove it from the fridge and roll with a rolling pin until it is very thin. Cut it into triangular pieces. Each triangle is rolled up with the ends curled in to make the croissant shape and then placed in the oven. Bake for ten to fifteen minutes and the result is hot, golden croissants.

Voila!—as any French *pâtissier* or pastry chef would say, except this was puff pastry—an intriguing area of specialized baking.

Hélène started to work, and I decamped to the garden. When I returned, she had just placed the tray of dough in the fridge and was cleaning up.

"Well, that went nicely. We should have some croissants in the morning," she said, satisfied with her morning's work.

The next day she lifted the tray from the fridge. "Oh," she said, poking at the dough. "Well, that didn't work."

I looked over her shoulder at the limp mass lying flat on the tray. The dough hadn't risen.

"Is there anything you can do with it?"

"No—nothing. I'll have to start over again. Puff pastry is a bitch," she said.

She lifted the tray over the garbage can and dumped the contents into it.

Preparations started again that morning, and the next day the dough had risen and was looking promising. By now I was beginning to feel a palpable anxiety coming from the kitchen as Hélène hoped to lift from the oven some perfectly light and flaky croissants that had risen gloriously like butterflies emerging from their cocoons. Instead, the pastry was heavy and tough. We made the best of it with lots of jelly and coffee, but we both knew something was wrong. After we taste-tested the first few, the rest were thrown out. The jar of red currant jelly that I had put out on the table with so much anticipation was returned to the fridge. I was tempted to buy croissants at the *boulangerie* while I picked up the *Trib* the next morning, but knew that would only confirm her failure.

While I was showering, Hélène telephoned Suzette next door and they met outside over the fence. A long conversation ensued, and Hélène went to the Intermarché, returning once again with the ingredients.

The morning passed without croissants to accompany the coffee and newspaper, and then the following day another batch of croissants was pulled from the oven. The golden colour and rich, fresh-baked smell alone told me these ones were different. Hélène was smiling. I was told they had to rest and could not be eaten straight from the oven.

They were worth the wait. I tore the crab claw off the end of one and ate it. And I did the same with the other end. And then I ate the rest of the croissant. The flaky, layered texture reached all the way to its moist core as it should—melting, mouth-watering and exquisite. By the time I reached for a third croissant, my wife was smiling in a way that was usually associated with a new mother.

"Exquisite. How did you do it?" I asked, tearing off the end and smothering it with red currant jelly. "Much better than anything I can buy in the village, even from those two ladies."

"They *are* good," she said modestly. "It's all in the kneading and the temperature of the dough."

"I can't wait to have croissants like this every morning," I said, thinking of *pain au chocolat* as well with its dark chocolate filling still warm from the oven.

"Oh, no! They're far too much work. You'll have to buy them in the village."

•   •   •

The bold clouds sailing across the sky were leading me as if I were part of their world and not the road I was riding on. The familiar copses, the farmhouses, a village along the way—all paled in importance to the strength and endurance I now felt that had been building in my lungs and my legs all spring. I reached the knoll of a small hill and slowed to look around before descending on a road that disappeared into a glade of trees. I knew that the road led to a bridge at the bottom that crosses a ravine and then rose up another hill on the far side. From the months of riding I had become familiar with the farms and had watched them change through part of the growing season. I also realized that I had changed as well.

At first I had ridden for physical conditioning and a sports outlet, then to explore the surrounding countryside. Now the rides had become a place to be alone and think. The act of pedalling had a cadence to it—like a heartbeat: always present yet easy to ignore. It had the effect of detaching me from my physical senses, leaving my mind free for other, larger thoughts. The hypnotic rhythm of riding caused the seemingly endless and sinuous back roads to straighten into one long ribbon before me. It was an illusion, of course, and I forced myself to stop for just a moment to put both feet on the ground, before continuing once more.

Chapter 9

creatures of all shapes and sizes ~ how to find the wild things

WHEN WE FIRST bought the villa and moved in, I had thought the garden devoid of creatures. At least, I rarely saw any, other than the odd butterfly or bird that passed through and a few small lizards that scurried into crevices whenever I approached. As we turned our attention to the garden, everything seemed still, even silent. I wondered about this, but we had renovating and furnishing on our minds for the first while. After that, we spent more time outdoors and slowly began to see the things we hadn't had time to notice. It wasn't a matter of just going out and looking either. We learned that living there brought us in contact with all sorts of things that only revealed their presence in accordance with the time of day or certain seasons of the year.

Myrtille, the neighbours' cat, was the first creature I got to know, but that was more a case of her finding us. It was the hunter in her that alerted me to what I had missed with my own eyes: the lizards she stalked; the mice and birds she dutifully brought in the house to show us; the squirrel she suddenly chased that wisely stayed high in the trees leaping branch to branch, causing them to sway as it made its way across the yard.

Gardening in Provence is a different experience from Vancouver. The soil is dry; roses escape the powdery mildew of a cool, moist climate and flourish with glossy green leaves; herbs grow wild and scent the air. With my head down as I worked, hours would pass in a pleasant way. The sheer peace of a project with no worries connected to it was seductive, and a garden had no end of tasks.

I had been trimming the rosemary hedge, sending the pungent resinous scent up my nose, when a small green twig caught my attention. It looked somehow out of place. On closer examination, I realized that a praying mantis was staring back at me, and it was unaware or uncaring of the danger I posed with my pruning shears. I studied the pale green frame of animated sticks, its triangular head and the vampire eyes of a creature waiting to dine on some passing insect or even the head of her mate. I could either continue pruning or let it get on with its business. It must have outstared me, for I left it there and went on with another chore.

With the return of warm weather, masses of valerian begin to flourish everywhere in Provence. It grows wild on rocky hillsides and alongside the roads. And it had even taken hold in the open spaces of our garden, growing taller each week until finally topping out with great clouds of pink blossoms. Having reached full bloom, it vibrated with the comforting hum of assorted visiting insects. Pairs of butterflies fluttered into the garden and then out again. The bumblebees lived up to their name, for, dressed like clowns in their furry black and yellow striped coats, they stumbled about, colliding randomly with the flowers that swayed and sagged under their added weight while they busily stuffed their sacks with pollen and careened drunkenly away again. Some ghostly apparitions silently arrived, making blurry dashes from flower to flower, and then were gone in a single flit. At first I thought they were hummingbirds, but on closer observation I realized they were hummingbird moths, one of those copycat crossover species. Then, the two doves we knew from the previous year were back, cooing contentedly, gliding through the trees, one always near the other.

I occasionally found the remains of black scorpions flattened under the mat at the front door, or worse, hiding beneath a shoe. If I disturbed one, it never stood its ground to fight but instead just scuttled away to seek a new place to hide. Myrtille played with them using quick, short passes with a paw, always careful not to touch or linger too close, as if she had already experienced their sting.

"*Gordon!*"

I heard the urgency and dashed to the front door to find my wife twisting her hands together and looking at the shoes she wore for gardening.

"What is it?"

"A scorpion! It's *there*," she said, pointing at the shoes.

I bent over and picked up one shoe expecting to find a huge scorpion with its tail menacingly raised and ready to strike. Instead, it was flattened on the doormat where the shoe had been.

"It's dead," I said.

"I know!" she grimaced. "I hit it with my shoe. Will *you* get rid of it?"

This wasn't normal, for she'd had plenty of experience with scorpions, having taken them on with an aggressive 'how dare you' attitude. I went into the garage, returning with a broom and dustpan to sweep up the flattened remains.

"Sorry. When I tried to put on my shoe I could feel it move—ugh. Remind me to shake out my shoes in the morning."

"Okay," I said gently.

"We need some lavender. Do you remember that movie *A Good Year*? The housekeeper put sachets of lavender on all the sills to keep scorpions out of the house."

From that day on the aroma of lavender filled the rooms. I would find it in the back of the closets, under the bed and armoires and behind the couch. Often these packets turned up in the middle of the floor after one of Myrtille's visits.

In the evening, geckos would cling high on the wall of the house by the light at the front door, waiting for insects to fly sufficiently close for capture. Myrtille, always the hunter, would sit below watching and waiting for a gecko to stray down the wall. Now and then she would stand on her hind legs and stretch up as high as she could reach with her forelegs as if measuring the distance to a gecko, but they inevitably remained just beyond that reach.

I began to realize there were things I might never see unless I was present at the right moment. One particularly hot day, Tabitha was hunting some creature on the face of the dry stone wall. I went over to investigate and found an iridescent green lizard over a foot in length that had pressed itself deeply into a crevice. The lizard wasn't going to budge and, as I watched,

Tabitha settled at the foot of the wall to wait it out. Later, I walked past to see that Tabitha had given up the hunt and had moved onto a pad of concrete to stretch out in the sun. Behind a large pillar on the same pad was the lizard.

Our garden turned out to be fertile hunting ground. The cats hunted the bigger things like birds and rodents. The geckos competed with the spiders and the mantises in the hunt for smaller insects. François said toads preferred flies and butterflies. The wasps devoured almost anything, alive or dead. Scorpions, whose stinging tails were only useful for defence, ate something, but I never learned what. Some insects preferred me as I often found, nursing bites on my arms and legs after gardening. Clearly the garden was a living, biting, consuming kind of place.

That first spring, I noticed strings of eggs floating in an open concrete water tank that was sunk into the garden. I was only there for a matter of weeks before I had to return to my law practice in Vancouver, so I missed whatever might have hatched in my absence.

Frogs—*grenouilles*—were famous as a tasty delicacy, probably first tried during a period of starvation when anything that moved or grew was eaten. I had heard that during the Second World War the Dutch ate tulip bulbs. In any event, I hadn't forgotten the strings of eggs.

A week earlier, I had bent over some miniature roses (which I had planted around the base of a tree) and noticed a stone half-buried in the ground that I hadn't seen before. Just as I was about to pick it up, it blinked at me. I froze in mid-reach and looked closer to see the stone heave slightly and blink again. But that was all it did. The toad stayed, seemingly quite secure, hidden in its layer of earth, legs folded beneath it as tranquilly as a Buddhist monk in meditation. It merely shifted again and blinked a few more times. I backed away and left it to its thoughts. When I returned the next day, it had already moved on, leaving just a small indentation in the soil.

If there was one, there had to be more. But when did they come out, and how did they survive, let alone meet up to procreate, in the subzero temperatures of winter and the hot, bone-dry days of summer? It had to have been one of those toads that would dig itself into the ground and remain there in a form of hibernation or suspended animation until the conditions were right for it to emerge once more.

Several weeks later we planned a dinner at a restaurant with friends. The weather had deteriorated that day so that rain had begun to fall before we left home. Fortunately, the restaurant had a charming, warm dining room and we enjoyed the evening. By the time we were ready to leave, however, the clouds had opened up and a heavy rain was falling. The windshield wipers were running at full speed, but visibility was difficult in the pounding rain with the dark road lit only by the headlights of the car. Reaching the bottom of the hill near home, I made the sharp turn and had begun the climb up the road to our house when I saw movement in the rain splashing off the surface road. It was as if the road had come alive and was shifting before my eyes. As I slowed the car, I could make out crouching, crawling and hopping creatures—and there weren't just a few, but hundreds.

I stopped.

"*Grenouilles?*" my wife murmured.

"I think they may be toads, not frogs," I replied in a hushed voice of awe.

"Don't drive—you'll kill them," she said, adding, "Where did they come from?"

I had no answer. We just sat in the car a while longer, looking out the windscreen at the moving surface of the road.

Finally she asked, "What are we going to do?"

"Well, we can wait, or we can walk. The house is just a hundred yards away."

Without waiting for a response, I backed to the side of the road, and we both got out of the car. The rain splashed up around our ankles. The toads were everywhere underfoot and constantly moving. We walked with our heads down to keep the rain from our faces and to watch where we were stepping. Busy in their festival, the toads were oblivious to our walking through their midst. By the time we made it to the house, we were dripping like wet mops, so we peeled off our clothes, towelled down and went to bed.

By morning the rain was over, so I walked down the hill to get the car. The toads were gone, their presence from the night before proven only by the odd one pancaked on the road by some passing car. After that, every time I walked through the trees of the ravine across from our house (now known as Toad Hollow), I thought about what I might be stepping on, hidden there waiting for the next rainfall or breeding season to come along. It occurred to me that although we had bought the villa and garden, these creatures were the real owners and inhabitants and would still be here long after we had moved on.

Tabitha had been a relatively distant cat, preferring to keep to herself. The previous year she would disappear into the neighbour's yard for long hours and not return until I would

88

go looking and calling for her. However, this year, when I was gardening or working on a stone wall, I would often turn and, to my surprise, find her sitting a few feet away watching what I was doing. If I moved to some other area thinking I had left her behind, it was just as likely that I would discover she had followed me and was watching again. She wasn't there to seek attention. She simply wanted to be nearby, keeping company. If I reached out to pet her, she would accept the attention; but if I tried to pick her up, she would move just a few feet farther off. Then something like a butterfly would attract her attention, and she would be off to investigate. Yet always she would return a short while later to watch once more what I was doing.

. . .

The fly made several circles over my head and then settled on the upper corner of the computer screen. I stopped typing to watch, amused at first. It left and returned, each time scribing circles in the air, staying in the warm ray of sunlight that bathed my desk by the open window. I tried to concentrate on my writing, but the fly landed on the screen once more and began following the new letters as I typed. I stopped, fingers on the keyboard, watching as it sat a moment longer and then flew out through the open window and into the sunshine. It seemed to be inviting me to join it.

I remained immobile, distracted. A hint of summer breeze passed through the window where I sat in shorts and a T-shirt trying to work, but my concentration had been broken. It had to be time to wash the car, I began thinking, so I went downstairs and opened the garage doors wide, uncoiled the hose and set to work.

"*Allô.*"

I turned to see Pierre Luc and his dog, Fidel, standing at our gate. He took my smile and wave as a welcome, so he opened the gate and the two of them walked up the driveway. I put down the hose and went into the garage to shut off the water. They followed me in, and after the ritual greetings he got to the point.

"I should start the *effeuillage* in the vineyard this week. Are you interested?"

"*Effeuillage?*" I asked.

He explained that it was the thinning of the leaves in order to let the sunlight reach the grape clusters. After a bit more discussion, I said I would be delighted to help. And then something happened that none of us was prepared for.

Myrtille was in the doorway to the staircase, standing on the tips of all four paws with her back arched and rigid, her black Siamese tail raised like a scorpion's barb ready to strike. Fidel saw her too, and his head immediately sank a few inches as he let out a low whine. Myrtille sidled forward like a crab, sizing up the situation. Fidel backed away, but unfortunately in the wrong direction, so that Myrtille's advance cut off his only escape out the garage doors. And then it all unravelled.

Letting out a deep moan, Fidel made a run for the open door to the guest suite with Myrtille in pursuit. I heard howls and the scuffling sounds of the chase, and by the time I got to the doorway, I saw them bound over the bed and begin a lap of the room, slipping and sliding as they crossed the tile floor. Fidel pushed off a couch and upended a chair in one corner. Next, he reached a tarpaulin, sending it and an open can of paint and tools flying. The lap around the room had given him what he must have wanted though, for he went back out the door and then on through the garage.

"What in . . . ?" Hélène exclaimed as she rushed in wearing her painting clothes. "Here, take the tarp out and hose it down. It's water-based paint. I'll mop up the floor." She acted before Pierre Luc or I could move. "Oh, *merde!* —there's even paint on the curtains. I'll wash them before it dries."

For once, Pierre Luc was at a loss for easy words. He attempted a Gallic shrug and then abandoned it. I looked around, taking in the dog prints crossing the rumpled bed and the couch, the upended chair and the paint soaking through the tarp. Pierre Luc started to help with the dripping tarp and, as we carried it outdoors, I saw Fidel far up the road, heading home. Myrtille was now sitting in the garage, composed, calmly cleaning herself.

Later, when I returned to my computer, so had the fly.

Chapter 10
on the road ~ searching for Provence

First, dressed in skins, rude, barbarian, the Ligures and Cavares our ancestors fought for the niggard soil, dwelling in caves of the mountain or the seashore; and with them were the fairy folk of the forest, the troglodytes of old, who cast their spells on life and swayed its counsels. Then came the galleys of the Greeks upon the cradling waters of the sparkling sea.

—Frédéric Mistral, writing of his own land

THE WINDOW WAS OPEN and sun streamed across the desk as my work on Provence took shape on the computer screen.

Legend has it that by 600 BCE Greek and Phoenician sailors appeared along the coast and founded Marseille. They navigated up the waterways, trading and introducing grapevines and fruit and olive trees that laid the seeds for the agrarian way of life we know in the Rhône Valley today. In time, their influence waned under the Roman military expansion that brought a very different order to the land. The Romans were far more than just another conqueror with an efficient military machine, for they arrived with an extraordinary sense of organization and an administrative system unseen before. They imposed a unified state, orderly government, an integrated and highly developed system of criminal and civil laws that covered property rights, inheritance, marriage, trade and commercial matters, an efficient postal system and a common currency that Europe would not see again until the *euro* was introduced in the late twentieth century. They were superb engineers and builders, erecting cities complete with running water and sewage systems; they invented concrete to build their great viaducts and theatres. Their roads were so well constructed that they remain visible today.

This stable environment, the *Pax Romana*, allowed the empire to function smoothly and the economy to thrive. When Rome finally fell in the fifth century AD, their civilization fell with it; their knowledge of engineering and administration was lost, leaving a void, a more primitive order where mysticism thrived, bands of brigands roamed, and small fiefdoms were staked out behind crude fortifications.

No matter where Hélène and I drove, even after the centuries of the Dark and Middle Ages, the Enlightenment, and innumerable conflicts and finally two world wars, there remains the physical presence of that empire. Travelling Provence today is a bit like finding, protruding from the earth, the bones of some long-extinct great prehistoric creature that have been scattered across the landscape. It is a reminder of what once thrived here. Tourists stop and look in awe and walk the ruins, and even enjoy operas and bullfights in ancient yet still functional Roman arenas and theatres that even today dominate many of the cities, towns and villages.

Something begins to happen to anyone who lives in Provence for very long. There is a splendour that warms the soul, a vast and diverse garden inseparable from the blue sky and the dazzling sun. By some sort of osmosis, the body and mind seem to absorb and become altered by the warmth of the sun and air and the relaxing way of life. Provence has an irresistible beauty that engenders a sense of isolation from the outside world as if it is a place unto itself—its own unique creation. One feels that life in Provence would function very well without all of our modern transportation, televisions, telephones, the Internet and even the watch on my wrist. Life here has its own sense of time and rhythm, seemingly self-sufficient and independent of everywhere else.

Quaint medieval villages perch on hilltops and walled villages like Richerenches, built by the Knights Templar, stand on open plains. The soil yields up Roman coins for treasure hunters armed with their metal detectors, and dogs are trained to dig for truffles, the valuable and edible 'black diamonds' of Provence. The village *librairies*, or bookstores, sell books written by local authors on the history and culture of their villages, and before new residents realize it, they are becoming '*provençalized*' in some way or another. We could sense it happening to us, little by little, as each day passed.

Provence continues today as it has for thousands of years. The older villagers we came to know can still speak the old *provençal* language, laced with words rooted in the language of the early Greek traders. The outdoor markets, a throwback to the old trading centres, fill the streets of the villages, towns and cities at least once each week. People can still, with a little trading, live off what they produce from farms passed down over generations. The barbarian invaders have been replaced by wealthier ones who arrive to buy up the old stone *mas* and ruins to rebuild them into summer villas with swimming pools and tennis courts. With the reliance on agriculture on the decline, these new invaders are attracted to the sunny climate and the casual lifestyle that is hard to find elsewhere. Provence has seen expatriates arrive for all of recorded time: from the northern barbarians who came by land, to the Greeks and Phoenicians who came by sea, to the Romans who came by the roads built for their legions, and now to the new expatriates arriving by international flights. It could be argued that Provence has not really changed at all.

As I typed, the fly had returned through the open window, and as this seemed to be a good place to take a break for the day, I pushed back my chair, rose from the desk and went out to the garden.

·   ·   ·

For us, Provence became the roads we travelled. We drove everywhere in search of its history or to drop in on some event we had heard of or read about in the local newspaper. Sometimes we would take trips to historical sites and beautiful villages that friends had recommended, or start out without any plan in mind, only to stumble on an event in a village.

"Let's see the cave art in the Ardèche today—or how about the Roman ruins in . . . ?"

As our wandering widened to take in more-distant sites, we planned our itinerary on a Michelin map. I was the pilot and drove the car; my wife was the co-pilot with the open map on her lap and one finger tracing the route.

One Sunday, amid endless green vineyards under an infinite blue sky, we were driving past the village of Cairanne and saw that there was a festival under way. We parked the car and began to walk up the hill to the village where a woman was standing at the side of the road beside a stack of cardboard boxes labelled *verres*.

"Would you like wine glasses?" she asked. "You will need them." She held out two glasses, which we took.

I read what was etched into my glass.

CAIRANNE
CÔTES DU RHÔNE VILLAGE

"Is there a wine tasting here today?"

"*Oui*, but also much more. This is the annual food festival for our village," she said, smiling back at me. "You will enjoy it."

We thanked her and continued up the hill and through the arch of an old stone portal where wood gates once hung, guarding entry to the village. We found ourselves in a milling crowd of people. Most had a Cairanne glass in one hand and food in the other. Stalls had been set up offering foods and wines to taste and all sorts of other things. A woman sold homemade jams and *pain d'épice*, a honey and spice bread, while her daughter played under the table.

One man demonstrably showed off how the garden shears he sold could ever-so-effortlessly lop a thick branch off a tree. "*Voilà!*" he hollered with every cut, and then raised the shears into the air for everyone to admire.

We had started the day thinking about a quiet drive before lunch. Instead, we were sipping wines in a crowded square before noon. Granted, the pours in our glasses were small; yet I had also learned that they added up all too quickly. Just the same, this was an opportunity to compare the local wines of Cairanne, Châteauneuf-du-Pape, Gigondas and more. *Be selective and try only the best*, I told myself. *Taste and use the pots nearby to spit; don't swallow*—which I had previously discovered was a necessary discipline.

In the midst of this activity a small parade of men in medieval costumes appeared from one of the narrow streets, hollering and banging on boards, cutting a path through the crowd. As they marched, some of them reached into sacks they were carrying and threw oranges into the crowd. I caught one, and then realized that a small boy next to me

97

had reached for it as well. I handed it to him. He smiled shyly at me and ran back to his mother to show his prize.

On another day, driving south through Sablet we found the town square filled with parasols sheltering tables piled high with books. Sitting at each table was a person, with a pen in hand, autographing books. We had landed at a book fair of local authors. I bought a biography of author and dramatist Marcel Pagnol from a young man who said he knew the Pagnol family. At another table an elderly man with a droopy moustache (wearing a tweed sports jacket in the midsummer heat) smoked his pipe and signed his mystery novels about a black tomcat called Tiburse that solved crimes for an incompetent detective.

Along the roads we drove, it seemed as if every other power pole had a poster tacked to it boldly announcing that *Circus Zavatta* was coming to town. It reminded me of the old Burma-Shave rhyming roadside ads advertising shaving products. However, *Zavatta* used only one phrase: *Zavatta is coming!* Even the rentable billboards carried this message. The more we drove, the more signs we saw. They were everywhere, no matter where we drove, always announcing that *Zavatta is coming!—Zavatta is coming!* In time we came to expect them, and we began to look forward to their arrival. But when? And where? We waited and watched in anticipation, but we never did see *Circus Zavatta*. That didn't seem to matter though, for we were constantly reminded that *Zavatta is coming!*

To the south of Nyons lie the canals and waterwheels of Isle-sur-la-Sorgue; there the silk industry flourished in the 18th and 19th centuries and made fortunes before cheaper products from Asia arrived and took over the market. Just east of Isle-sur-la-Sorgue is the Fontaine de Vaucluse—a massive resurgence of water that wells from deep underground, fed by the rain that falls on the Plateau de Vaucluse and filters down through the fractured rock. In English it is called a *spring*, but in French it is a *source*—a far more evocative word as, metaphorically speaking, water is considered to be a source of life. Divers who have tried to plumb the spring had to give up at incredible depths; instead they found coins lodged in the walls of the spring dating back to the Romans. The water flows at a staggering 820 million cubic metres per year, creating the largest resurgence in Europe, forming its own river flowing west to the canals of Isle-sur-la-Sorgue and then out onto the plain of the Rhône Valley, where it eventually joins the Rhône River. It was here that Abélard wooed his Héloïse.

As we sped south to Avignon alongside the Rhône River, scullers were almost keeping pace with our car as they rowed downstream with the current. Beyond the scullers, on Ile de la Barthelasse, the red parasols over the tables of Restaurant Le Bercail came into view; from our distance, they looked like oversized poppies dotted along the riverbank. At a bend in the road, the ramparts of Avignon came into view, and then the four remaining arches of the Pont d'Avignon that once extended to the far shore, and now, like a severed arm, only reaches partway across the water.

A freight barge chuffed slowly upstream against the river, its black hull in relief against the silted water. On deck a young girl played with her dog; in the wheelhouse stood a man who was probably her father; in the kitchen below would be the mother, no doubt preparing lunch. We had been told that the family-operated barge industry was dying a natural death as more goods were being transported by the faster methods of rail and semitrailers. All the same, recent studies have shown that a barge can carry far more at lower cost with less ecological impact than the newer forms of transportation. However, by the time this is fully appreciated the family barge industry will likely be extinct as a way of life.

When the Roman papacy fractured into two schisms in the fourteenth century, one seat of power moved to Constantinople and the other to Avignon, where it remained for seven decades. The Avignon papacy controlled Avignon as well as an area known as the Comtat Venaissin, roughly the same area as today's Vaucluse *département* or district. It extended along the east side of the Rhône River from Cavaillon in the south to Bollène and Vaison-la-Romaine in the north. The popes had built a grand palace on a knoll in Avignon and lived opulent lives; however, they discovered that armed power was the real ruling force of the day when a French officer and knight, Bertrand du Guesclin, brought his army to the walls of the city, demanding two hundred thousand francs for his military campaigns. When Pope Urban V offered to buy him off by levying a special tax on the population, Guesclin refused the money until the papacy paid the ransom from its own purse.

We arrived in Avignon in time for lunch and walked from the river through the gates in the great wall and along busy streets to Place de l'Horloge at the centre of the city. As ever, at one end of the Place, the merry-go-round in front of the dollhouse opera theatre was spinning in a kaleidoscope of bright colours and broadcasting circus music beneath the canopy of leaves to the cafés that teemed with diners and scurrying waiters.

The Place, with its gothic clock tower, acts as a hub from which streets radiate out like crooked spokes in a broken wheel, until they touch the very ring of defence walls that still encompass old Avignon. The novelist Lawrence Durrell lived in a cottage nearby, where he wrote his exotic *Avignon Quintet,* set in the nineteen-thirties and forties. One of his characters was an insomniac who walked the city at night, avoiding the areas he thought too dangerous in the dark. Durrell wrote of him being importuned by a child prostitute, a Gypsy, who lived in a squalid shack built against the outer walls of the city that Gypsies were not permitted to enter.

As it happened, this was July and the Festival d'Avignon was underway, so Place de l'Horloge was alive with actors, clowns, mimes and more, all dressed in theatrical costumes and doing short skits to draw people into their theatres. We had lunch under the trees at a café where a pair of Charlie Chaplins cavorted about, handing out leaflets. Then a young woman dressed as a clown arrived and, with a delightful smile, entertained the people dining at tables in the hope of earning tips. I smiled back at her and gave her a tip before she moved on. She seemed to be enjoying herself, and we enjoyed her moment with us. My tip had been on the small side as we had already been approached by others and expected even more before we finished lunch. Later, as we strolled a side street, I noticed the same girl, now sitting on the pavement, her mask off, with a look of dejection on her face. I thought of the trivial amount I had given her, realizing that even the work of a clown was not all happiness.

Arles was once a strategic seaport for the Greeks and Phoenicians, who arrived by the Mediterranean and then navigated up the Rhône River into the heart of the country to settle and trade their goods. In their turn, the Romans built their capital of Gaul at Arles and stayed for centuries. However, after several thousand years of sediment washing down the river into the ever-expanding delta known as the Camargue, Arles lost its strategic importance and became an inland city; yet it is so layered with the trappings of its Roman past that it is now designated a UNESCO World Heritage Site.

We stayed several days in a hotel with a glass floor in the lobby that revealed excavated Roman ruins metres below. Arles remains a city of of time-honoured costumes and iridescent silks and lace, still worn at festivals, of *ferias* with bullfights in which the bulls are no longer killed. Christian Lacroix carried his love for the flamboyance and bright colours from his youth in Arles all the way to the *haute couture* runways of Paris.

If their photos were placed side by side, they could easily be mistaken for one another, for Buffalo Bill Cody and Frédéric Mistral shared many things. Both wore their hair long, had goatees and wore broad-brimmed hats; both became legendary figures for depicting the way of life they knew. Cody received a Medal of Honor for service to the U.S. Army as a scout; Mistral was a Nobel laureate in literature. One was born in 1846, the other in 1830, in times when their countries were in transition. They met in Provence when Cody was touring Europe with his Wild West Show. One used a gun, the other a pen; one was a celebrated showman, the other a gifted writer. One died in 1917, the other in 1914. Both championed a way of life.

Cody made the world aware of a disappearing era in the taming of the West. Mistral devoted his life to protecting the Occitan (Provençal) language of Languedoc (langue d'Oc) and the *troubadours* from a French government determined to create a single language in France. As a boy, he saw his parents embarrassed for not knowing French and he became fixed on preserving his culture. He wrote *Mireille*, his masterpiece of poetry in Occitan, compiled a dictionary in that language and endowed, with his Nobel Prize winnings, the Arlésien Museum containing Provençal art, furniture, costumes and farm equipment from that period.

The Wild West was tamed, Occitan and the culture it embodied shut out. Both men saw the world they grew up in become lost to the changes of time; both lived to see a new century and another era, theirs having passed them by.

One night while walking back to our hotel after dinner, we had just passed the statue of Frédéric Mistral in the Place du Forum when I stopped abruptly, for I realized I was looking at a scene I knew well. Taken by surprise, it was several moments before I grasped that we were standing on the very spot where Van Gogh had set up his easel and painted one of his most famous canvases, *The Café Terrace at Night*. The great awning reached out across the terrace, and people sat talking and drinking at tables lit by yellow artificial light, with the dark sky and stars behind.

Van Gogh had arrived in Arles in 1888 with the hope that his friend Paul Gauguin would join him and they would paint together. Gauguin did, but they soon quarrelled and he left, leaving Van Gogh to paint his greatest works. Genius often displays itself in just a few canvases, but not with Van Gogh, who had found his form in brilliant colours and bold brush-strokes that reached far beyond the known norms of art, all bursting with the raw energy and tormented emotions he felt in life. Despite several mental breakdowns in the last twenty months of his life, he produced some seventy paintings. By July 29, 1890 he had died of a gunshot wound near Auvers, north of Paris. Whether he shot himself out of despair or someone shot him is an open debate. Yet, on seeing his self-portrait and his acute measuring gaze, it is hard to believe that he was mad at all—just a manic, fragile man who had found his own artistic insight and was driven to express it.

Hélène had a different take on it. "Why would he paint bursting stars? The man must have been nearsighted."

The rock on which Les Baux rests resembles a beached ship, the ruins of the ancient village forming the superstructure along its crest. The ghostly ruins of Les Baux, built so strategically on a remote outcrop to the west of St-Rémy, give little indication that this was once the centre of an empire with family and political ties to royalty as far off as Spain and Italy. This can be a haunting place, even in the full Provençal sun. After it was annexed to France in the fifteenth century, the king turned his cannons on it, reducing it to rubble, and thereby ending any chance of its recovery as a political force. Today, Les Baux is a heap of broken stone and shattered walls, with staircases that rise into the air and lead nowhere. I walked to the very tip and highest point on the promontory and found a catchment system for gathering rainwater carved into the smooth rock slope. I looked, but the cisterns that once stored the water must have long since disappeared. Les Baux, under the protection of the Ministry of Culture, is now a tourist destination. Buses park by the road in designated stalls to disgorge tourists for a swift two-hour photo stop, before they are gathered up again and moved on for lunch at a predetermined nearby restaurant.

We stood staring in awe at the Pont du Gard, rising fifty-five metres above the river in order to span an entire valley, with its three tiers of arches glowing orange in the afternoon sun. It is difficult to find another artefact that shows so clearly the Roman presence in Provence. It was built in the first century AD from blocks of stone weighing as much as six tons cut from a nearby quarry. The massive edifice formed part of an aqueduct some fifty kilometres in length to carry water to the city of Nîmes. On seeing it, the first thing that came to mind was that the Romans must have believed they were building for all eternity.

In Nîmes the Romans built an amphitheatre, the Maison Carrée, and a bathhouse that reveal the opulence of their way of life. Today the *ferias*, drawing some 22,000 spectators into the Roman arena, offer tame versions of bullfights twice each year. The magnificent Jardin de la Fontaine is a wonder of stone and water.

The people living nearby have become accustomed to these structures that they pass each day as they go about their business. We heard of one farmer caught casually picking stones out of a section of the Roman aqueduct that crossed his property for the barbeque he was building in his yard. When an archaeologist admonished him, he seemed surprised to learn that the stones he took so much for granted were part of a historically protected monument.

Feeling tired after an afternoon of driving, I turned to my wife. "Have we seen enough?"

"Yes, let's go home. I'm saturated with all this stuff."

So we drove back to Nyons, past more power poles that announced *Zavatta is coming!*

Chapter 11
the city of fountains

. . . and the song of multiple fountains, which one discovers with enchantment in the fresh silent shade of the courtyards and gardens, where dolphins and bearded gods blow water into their deep beautiful basins.

— Martial and Braive, *Aix-en-Provence*

BEYOND THE SHEER JOY and verve for life that makes Aix-en-Provence so vibrant, I had another motive for visiting again. Over two millennia ago several pivotal battles happened there and I wanted to see where they had taken place.

Rather than the autoroute from Nyons to Aix and its wild river of traffic, we decided on the quieter *département* roads and a leisurely day's drive in the countryside.

Rising early, we headed south to Vaison-la-Romaine, then followed the D938 to Carpentras before switching to the D4 leading east to the Plateau de Vaucluse and its forest of scrub trees and rock outcroppings. From there we descended onto the level plain of the Lubéron Valley, a countryside that makes superb postcard material. Protected historic villages nestle into the hillsides while chic, well-tended villas with obligatory swimming pools lie casually scattered across the landscape.

In the middle of the valley, between Gordes and Apt, the village of Roussillon rests atop a spectacular formation of bright ochre that was once mined and used as a colouring agent for stucco and paint. We drove up a curving road through a pine forest, arriving late and without a reservation at Restaurant David, which sits on a bluff jutting out precariously from the hilltop. Luck fell our way, for the waiter had one remaining table by a window, giving us a panoramic view of the Lubéron Valley.

I had sea bass with sabayon sauce and diced summer vegetables, and Hélène had scallops on a bed of buttered spinach. We shared dessert while watching tourists below whose shoes turned different shades of red and orange as they wandered in and out of the ochre quarries. One of the books I had read on Provence reported that the ochre miners had burrowed beneath sections of the village, rendering some buildings unsafe for occupation.

I had also read that at the end of the last war, the French Resistance fighter Raoul Chanon, in his new role as head of the commune of Roussillon, had received a telegram from the recently formed liberation government of France ordering him to arrest twelve of the villagers.

"*Nous réglons nos affaires en famille*"—We take care of things inside our family, he said, tearing up the telegram. The act made him an instant hero.

We rose from lunch that afternoon to drive south through the Lubéron, the countryside author Peter Mayle had made famous in his books about the valley. He had become a celebrity and then was hounded by acquaintances and gawking tourists, until finally he had enough, sold his villa and moved to a more secluded location. His books became so popular he almost single-handedly turned the area into a tourist destination. The locals may have disliked the change it brought to their peaceful valley, but they also appreciated the money that was left behind. I felt the urge to look up where he lived and drop in just to say hello, but I managed to suppress it and we continued on our way.

Bonnieux, mounted high on the hillside on the southern edge of the valley, serves as a gatekeeper to a road carved through a narrow gorge that makes its way across Montagne du Lubéron and eventually to Aix. And so, for six tortuous, serpentine kilometres, we wound our way behind a slow-moving car towing a trailer and finally emerged at Lourmarin, where Winston Churchill stopped between wars to paint its *château*. We circled the *château* and then lit out for Cadenet, crossed the Durance River and found the D17 that gave access to Aix by the back door—only to find we had arrived just in time for the five-o'clock rush hour. Our pace slowed to a crawl.

Unlike Avignon, the medieval walls that once encompassed Aix have long since been replaced by a road that runs counter-clockwise around the old village. Drivers traversing the city must join in a large merry-go-round. After a lot of creeping and idling, and with our conversation reduced to a standstill as well, we reached the great circular intersection of La Rotonde only to find that at this time of day it was a stalled vortex of traffic that behaved like a crush of anxious turtles. A rasping Vespa squeezed alongside our car, swerved in front of a bus and disappeared through the immoveable metal ahead. Cyclists, risking skin and bone, were doing the same thing. All the while, we watched La Rotonde, the grand fountain in the middle of the intersection, where half-drowned cherubs rode on the backs of swans and great streams of water blew into the air.

When we had arrived for our first stay in Aix the year before, the woman we were renting the apartment from had said on the phone that we would never find the place by ourselves. She gave us specific directions on where we should meet.

"Find the fountain at La Rotonde and then drive the length of Cours Mirabeau."

So we had driven up the Cours, avoiding the rambling pedestrians, and reached a small fountain set in the middle of the boulevard that we drove around. A bit further along, we came to a second fountain (also in the middle of the boulevard) and finally a third one set at the feet of a statue of King René, who had spent the last century or two looking down into the bubbling water. A building brought the Cours to an end, but a narrow street ducked around one side and led to a street we were told would take us to Place de Verdun, where she would be waiting.

All this seemed rather haphazard. How were we to recognize each other, and what would we do if we missed a turn along the way? Nevertheless, when we reached the Place there stood a woman in the crowd waving to us. She had to have identified us as a couple driving a leased car by our license plate. She climbed into the back seat, introduced herself, and then guided us down a series of narrow one-way

110

streets until we stopped in front of a huge set of wooden gates that must have once been a carriage entrance.

"Don't worry about the car—there's nowhere else to leave it," she said.

So we left it in the middle of the narrow street and carried our luggage up a once-grand circular staircase to the living quarters above. When we came back down, a line of vehicles had formed, the drivers patiently or not so patiently waiting for our return.

That was last year. I became attentive to the traffic once more as we cleared La Rotonde and vehicles were moving again.

We opened the tall shutters and windows in the apartment to let light and fresh air into the rooms. Nothing had changed, except the room looked dustier and the furniture more worn. The house, once an upper middle-class home with grand and well-proportioned rooms, had long ago been carved up into five or six small apartments. Our apartment had been the drawing room.

We unpacked and showered in the tiny bathroom cubicle shoehorned into what was once a vestibule closet. I stepped out of the bathroom in order to towel down and gazed around at the high ceiling, ornate mouldings and the two defunct marble-clad fireplaces at opposite ends of the room. The tall windows had shutters on the inside as well as outside. A false wall had been built to create a small bedroom at one end. Dusty and broken-up as it was, the room still had a charm and elegance that had drawn us back for this second stay.

Aix is a city that draws plenty of writers who foolhardily test their skills at describing its character. It rests in its green countryside unruffled due to the treed hills to the north that shelter it from the full force of the mistral wind and Mont Ste-Victoire rising to the east. Aix feels unhurried, as it is just far enough away from Marseilles as well as the arterial auto routes and TGV high-speed rail system that move millions of people annually between the Côte d'Azur and the rest of France. Its towering plane trees provide a significant reprieve from the intense Provençal sun that shines an average of three hundred days a year.

The suburbs that surround Aix are like any other: modern, efficient and dull. However, once freed from its medieval walls, its girdle removed, the worn old girl found a renewed vigour and growth.

Aix is also one vast promenade that begins on Cours Mirabeau and spreads through the city like a nervous system, past the shops, apartments, businesses and law courts, to the squares, *bistrots* and cafés that form gathering places for the outdoor lifestyle. The city pulsates, only resting briefly late at night before starting up again at dawn the following day. Step out on the street and you enter a living organism of *fêtes* and outdoor *marchés*, student events from the assorted universities and *manifestations* that are a regular part of French life. There are about 143,000 Aixois. However, in the tourist season that figure expands by twenty per cent. Aix has three universities that enrol some 70,000 students each year, as well as a military academy. The military presence is not new, for it extends all the way back to Gaius Sextius, who built a Roman outpost at the hot springs that are still in use today.

Few drivers care to venture inside the narrow streets of the old city, where delays are common and movement unpredictable, and this has made Aix a perambulator's dream.

All the same, there are hazards to this activity until one learns to look down, as well as up at the sights. For some inexplicable reason, humans have a primordial connection to other animals, and in France that connection is with dogs. They come in all sizes and colours, live in townhouses and apartments with their doting owners, and, on their least demand, are taken out onto the streets for a stroll.

These dogs check out other dogs, wait patiently while their owners shop, dine in restaurants (sometimes with their own chairs) and, of course, leave markers of their passing. Clearly, Aix has not yet passed the ordinances that Paris has to keep the streets safe for women's shoes and sandals, let alone bare feet. We passed a woman standing stork-like on one leg, the other raised as she looked at the sole of her patent leather pump that was encrusted with the fresh deposit of some Fifi or Samson.

"*Merde!*" she said angrily, following up more words that hung blue in the air.

Left long enough, these little markers dry, turn slowly to dust and are forgotten in the heat of the day.

The Office de Tourisme boasts that there are some forty fountains in Aix, for when these fountains were constructed the luxury of running water in residences had not yet even been contemplated. I lit out like a child on an Easter egg hunt to find as many as possible. Not that I walked every street and narrow chaotic lane in the city—but enough to have made a good try. The easiest to find were the ones in the squares or *places*. After that the search dwindled off, for I soon tired of the exercise as the effort began to outweigh the rewards. It's amazing to see just how much water the Aixois have to play with.

The best way to enter old Aix is to start at the Fontaine de la Rotonde and stroll the entire length of Cours Mirabeau. The Cours sets the stage as a grand portal, serving to enchant visitors from the moment they arrive. The fountain, with its three tiers of water basins, is thirty-two metres in diameter. Twelve marble lions guard dolphins, and cherubs ride the backs of bronze swans, all spouting water into the air. Viewed from overhead, the Rotonde and the Cours together form a giant exclamation mark that seems to proclaim: *I AM AIX!*

Despite the fact that the city was founded by the Romans around the hot springs of Sextius, there is remarkably little Roman architecture remaining today, with none of the amphitheatres and victory arches that dominate other cities in France. As a result, Aix has its own unique harmony, rhythm and style.

Most weekends, the great canopy of leaves on the Cours becomes a vast circus tent 440 metres long where all kinds of events, from fairs and festivals to outdoor expositions and parades, take place. One day it morphed into a market where I came across a couple selling truffles. The price was so low I asked why. The man explained they were white *truffes* from Mont Ventoux, not the more costly black variety. All the same, the great flatulent nose escaping the sealed glass containers they were stored in was just as pungent. I bought, putting the small glass jar in my pocket. Later, I was told there were no white truffles in France, so they likely came from China.

Aix is a city of both the past and the present with its aging buildings from different eras and monuments of famous men long gone as well as its streets overflowing with the vibrant youths who spill out as refreshingly as the water from its aging fountains.

University students relaxed at tables on the restaurant patios, practising at being '*branché*', or cool, and oblivious to others, blowing blue tendrils of cigarette smoke in the air to curl across the noses of people seated nearby. Just the same, their backpacks filled with books gave away their goals and optimism. These were not the unfocused and unemployed youths I saw in other places.

Another day we saw two lines of young people marching down the centre of the Cours. One line was dressed in smart military uniforms; the other, in perfect parallel to the first, wore white rags that reminded me of Egyptian mummies that had come to life. They marched past where we were standing and on to Fontaine la Rotonde. The ones in uniforms stopped the traffic and surrounded the fountain as if guarding it like the lions that were already there. Meanwhile, the mummies climbed into the lowest pool and stood under the gushing streams of water, raised their arms in some sort of celebration and then cavorted excitedly about knee-deep in water. When they finally dispersed, I asked a young lady wearing one of the uniforms what it was all about.

"We've just graduated from the engineering college and this is our party," she informed me.

The next morning some of them were still on the Cours, looking exhausted from their all-night partying. In a café, the same young lady was sleeping with her head on the shoulder of one of the only mummies who had not changed out of his wet clothing. A couple, still in their uniforms, were walking hand-in-hand, which drew raucous cheers from the others.

Strolling the length of the Cours we window-shopped the fashion boutiques, explored the narrow aisles of a French bookstore and read the posted menus of the restaurants.

People met and there was always a spare moment for a glass of *vin* or a *bière* or perhaps even a *pastis* or two at a table under the plane trees. Above all this activity the shuttered or curtained windows of hotel rooms and private apartments.

Cars crawled slowly about the narrow streets, like unwelcome animals that had found themselves out of their element, competing unsuccessfully with the pedestrians.

Aix is a city for walking. Every street corner brings its own surprises, possibly a new undiscovered square where there may be another weekly market of some sort underway. And when the market is over for the morning, the *bistrot* tables and umbrellas once again spread out beneath the trees with gaggles of crows socializing noisily overhead. There is more outdoor activity in Aix than we ever imagined from our earlier stay. Large markets where anything may be found swing into operation on Place de Verdun and the abutting Place des Prêcheurs. Then there is Place Richelme, where the steady flow of conversations at the outdoor tables vies with the clink of cutlery and glasses, lasting late into the night. By dawn, the same space has magically transformed into a food market. The citizens of Aix seem to pass their time outdoors, only retiring to their rooms to make love and sleep before each dawn brings another sunny day.

The grey and worn facades of the buildings do not reveal what may lie inside. Behind the closed doors are some of the most extraordinary examples of frescos and *trompe l'oeil* in rooms that have remained unaltered from when they were built centuries ago. I lurked by the doors of several famous addresses, waiting for someone to enter or leave so that I could glimpse inside. The intricate wrought-iron railings of the staircases that I managed to see hinted at what lay beyond. I never did succeed at mounting the stairs to the private rooms to see for myself.

After Cézanne died, the art curators of Aix turned away his art as being too *nouveau*. For them, artistic realism was still the vogue. A few blocks from our apartment we passed a plaque on the wall of a house that read: 'DANS CETTE MAISON EST MORT LE 23 OCTOBRE 1906 PAUL CEZANNE'. It was there in the house of his doctor that Cézanne died.

At night the city changes, bathed within the glow of artificial lights that push back the sense of mystery that comes with darkness. At night our instincts felt closer to the surface, our moods more pronounced. People dressed differently, acted differently, moved differently and talked differently. Once the chic boutiques had closed for the day the clothing in the windows became displays of fantasy wear, the stuff of dreams. During one of our perambulations, we accidentally strolled into a narrow, poorly-lit back street where young men and ladies waited in the shadows of doorways, like mannequins of the night selling other goods. They were not interested in us as a couple walking through We picked up our pace, saying little as we passed.

The restaurant Les Deux Garçons on the Cours dates from the 18th century, and is haunted by the ghosts of famous people. In the imaginations of tourists, Cézanne, Picasso, Hemingway and Zola still dine at the tables, although more wistfully than in the past. We decided to have dinner there one evening and then move on for *digestifs* on Place de Verdun next to the law courts in the centre of the city. This was convenient as, from the apartment, we had to pass through the Place on the way to Cours Mirabeau.

When we reached the Place, a girl and a boy were playing a game around the trunks of the plane trees. She was about eleven years of age and the boy a few years younger. Probably brother and sister judging by how they played, they were giggling and dashing about, touching each other in turns. The girl, trying to escape the boy's lunge, dashed across in front of us and broke our stride.

"*Tu es une gosse*"—a frisky child, Hélène said.

The girl swung around from her play and gave my wife a sassy look, yet all the same she seemed to like the unexpected attention. The boy stopped too.

"*Et moi?*" he asked, wanting a name as well.

Hélène looked at him for a moment. "*Un gamin*"—an urchin, she finally said.

Flattered by this new-found sense of identity, he broke out into a broad, self-conscious grin.

Their game interrupted, they now wanted our attention. We began walking again, but they tagged along, cheeky as street children. The girl was asking my wife questions in a quick dialect that was more like children's wordplay. Hélène picked up on this and tossed it back at her in the same playful manner. The boy pranced along half-listening. They followed us out of the Place and down a series of twisting narrow streets until we emerged on Cours Mirabeau. When we reached the restaurant, the *maitre d'* was waiting. The children knew their game with us was over, and we waved at them as they walked away.

It was a balmy evening and the Cours was busy with people, so we were fortunate to be placed at a table near the edge of the terrace where we could watch the activity. We ordered apéritifs to unwind and to decide on our plans for the next few days. The waiter brought the *apéros* and left menus with us, and then did not return to take our orders until he saw our empty glasses. The wine came first. It was a peppery red Gigondas that we sipped languidly with the appetizer dishes and then the main courses, only finishing the bottle before dessert arrived. When it was eventually time to leave, the evening had turned to night. We took the same route back up the narrow streets toward Place de Verdun, when suddenly the two children leapt out in front of us.

"*Zow!*" the girl said, and the boy copied her—"*Zow!*"

Hélène feigned surprise and then asked if it wasn't a bit late for the two of them to be out.

"*Non,*" the girl snapped in reply. With that they gambolled off together toward the Cours we had left just minutes earlier.

We walked on to Place de Verdun for the *digestifs* we had planned, only to find the children already waiting there. They were grinning like two Cheshire cats that had just swallowed their prey. This time we were startled. Clearly they knew the route we would take, but we had no idea how they'd gotten there before us.

"*D'où sortez-vous les enfants?*"—Where did you come from? my wife demanded.

The girl just shrugged her shoulders as if there was nothing to it. I could see getting more information out of her now would be impossible; she wasn't about to give away the secret of her little coup. The two giggled again with this gambit they had won, and fled like moths into the night—leaving us with their riddle.

Two days later we were again on Cours Mirabeau and out of curiosity I began a search for another street that could have led to Place de Verdun. I found nothing other than an uninterrupted wall of buildings, each abutting the next. When I was about to give up, Hélène nudged me and pointed at a steady stream of people coming and going through an arched doorway. Out of curiosity we entered, to find ourselves in a narrow covered passageway. As we walked along, squeezing our way past other people, the corridor widened slightly and sky appeared overhead. After walking a distance, we ascended a set of stairs that were covered overhead, and then abruptly we stepped out of the passageway and found ourselves standing in a treed square teeming with people.

For a moment I had no idea where we were, and then I recognized the café where we had stopped for *digestifs* the previous night. We had moved all the way from Cours Mirabeau to the center of Aix. It was as if we had been transported by a wormhole, straight from science fiction, that moves people great distances without any transition between places that are worlds apart. We had just found Passage Agard.

Chapter 12
Aix-en-Provence and its countryside

JUST A FEW MINUTES drive from the stone buildings and labyrinthine streets of Aix lie hillsides covered with pine forests. The transition happens so quickly you are struck by the fact that Aix is a small island surrounded by a greater countryside. In the rolling hills to the west is Club Set, where locals play tennis on red clay courts or just relax with a drink by one of the swimming pools. To the east, at the foot of Mont Ste-Victoire, are the stone quarries of Bibemus that Cézanne came to paint, and the village of Le Tholonet, which must look as it did a century ago.

Mont Ste-Victoire, rising behind, resembles a wedge of cheese cut from a giant round and laid on its side. The north face is a treed slope rising gently from the Infernet Valley to a peak of just over a thousand metres. The south face, or heel of the cheese, is a steep, massive white wall of crumbling stone rising boldly out of the landscape that extends from east to west for over twenty kilometres. It serves as a beacon for travellers on the A8 and the high-speed TGV rail system that form rivers of traffic across Provence to the playgrounds of Cannes and Nice—reminding them as they pass that Aix lies nearby. Yet somehow Aix is just far enough away from these arterial routes to rest in its own valley, as if part of another, more tranquil, world.

I wanted to return to Aix to trace its history back to the Romans. Searching for evidence of their presence, we stopped at the thermal baths of Aquae Sextae, built by the consul Sextius 2,200 years ago, when togas and broadswords were still *de rigeur* and the Romans were still losing their battle with the Celts. The village that grew around these baths became known by the contraction of Aquae Sextae into 'Aix'. We dropped by to find a thoroughly modernized facility that bore little resemblance to what the Romans once enjoyed. It turned out to be a sleepy place, as pale and flaccid as the old and moribund it catered to who were melting in its steaming mineral waters.

Inspired by the Roman history of the region, I wanted to climb Ste-Victoire and stand on its summit to look west to Aix and east to the battlefield at Pourrières. I stopped at the tourist office by Fontaine de la Rotonde and picked up a hiking map for the mountain. Hélène bought a fresh *baguette*, *charcuterie* and *pâté*, a selection of cheeses, a thermos for coffee and a bottle of rosé that she wrapped in layers of newspaper to keep cool. We packed our backpacks that night so that we would be ready to start out in the early morning. I had studied the map and we had decided to take the D10 along the Infernet Valley, park at Les Cabassols, and make the ascent from there.

We had imagined a romantic climb, starting at dawn on the gentle north slope as the night sky would begin to brighten with imperceptible shades of blue. The instructions on the trail map indicated it was an easy climb of about two hours; first through trees, then along a path that steepened when it broke out onto more barren terrain for the final ascent to the Cross of Provence at the summit. We could explore the priory built just below the cross and hike along the ragged cliff face to see the Garagaï. Reputedly the view took in the whole of Provence in one great panoramic vista, as far north as Mont Ventoux, the entire Rhône delta with a glimpse of the Mediterranean and east as far as the Côte d'Azur. This would be a perfect vantage point for an early lunch and then an easy descent along the crest of the mountain to the Bimont Dam.

We were late by the time we reached the starting point near Les Cabassols. The sun had already risen as we lifted the backpacks onto our backs and hiked over to the sign marking the trail. There was a notice tacked to it: '*Fermé! —risque d'incendie!*'

"All the trails on Ste-Victoire are closed due to a risk of forest fires," I said in amazement. "The woman at the tourist office didn't tell me this."

"Did you specifically ask her if the mountain was open for hiking?"

"Well, no—I just asked for a map of the mountain."

"There's the problem. The French are reluctant to volunteer information. That's considered presumptuous. They only answer exactly what you ask."

Neither of us said anything for some moments.

"Now what? We've got the whole day and a picnic packed."

We simply began driving, east along a deserted country road in the Infernet Valley with the north slope of Ste-Victoire on our right, past Vauvenargues where Picasso is buried and on toward more deserted terrain where the pine forest thins and is replaced by scruffy vegetation and rocky outcroppings. Ste-Victoire was soon behind us. Then, just when the road seemed to be leading us into the wilderness, we reached an intersection with another small road.

"Go south. We should be able to get around the end of the mountain from there."

The road descended through broken rock outcroppings until we reached level and open ground where I saw a sign.

"Pain de Munition!" I said.

"What?"

"That sign—Pain de Munition. This is where Marius and his soldiers defeated the Teutons. We must be near the battlefield."

We looked as we drove, to see only trees and peaceful green fields. There was no visible trace of the seminal battle that changed history.

Over two thousand years ago, in 124 BCE, Aix was at the frontier of the Roman Empire and prey to barbarian hordes numbering in the hundreds of thousands that soon arrived from the north and were moving, like swarms of locusts, in waves across the south of what is now Europe. They pillaged as they passed, destroying crops and animals that had been introduced by the Phoenicians and the Greeks, and disrupting the social order of the countryside. Often referred to as Celts, this massive migration of peoples was actually made up of a host of tribes: Cimbri, Teutons and others. Taller than the Romans and fierce beyond courage, the barbarians were known to chain themselves together and work themselves into a blind frenzy before fighting with a crazed intensity. Any who fled the battle line were killed as cowards by their own women.

The Celts' invincible strength and ferocity were legendary, for they defeated the Roman legions in almost every battle. In 105 BCE near Orange, the Romans reportedly lost nearly eighty thousand men. The soldiers were demoralized and fearful of another encounter. By 103 BCE the barbarians seemed headed into Italy to sack Rome, so the Romans sent some sixty thousand men under the command of Gaius Marius to stop them.

Marius was small in stature and had been a common legionnaire from a poor and obscure family. He first distinguished himself in hand-to-hand combat and was known as a rough, hard man, warlike by training and violent by disposition; yet he was patient and unusually tenacious. Trained by a military that favoured the patrician class for advancement, he nevertheless rose to become a general. Instead of indulging in the perks of office like other generals, he worked and fought with the soldiers in the field and shared their harsh lifestyle. He knew that his soldiers feared the barbarians, so he kept at a distance, avoiding battle to give his men time to observe the Celts and learn their ways, thereby slowly building the confidence of his men.

When he felt his army was ready, Marius surprised the Ambrones near Aix and took advantage of their disorganized state to defeat them. Then, in just a few days, he moved his army to the other side of Ste-Victoire where he chose a hill on the plain of Pourrières for another battle. There, he ordered his men to interlock their shields and hold their position.

Then, he goaded the Teutons to attack. So incited, they took the challenge and struggled uphill. Unable to gain a foothold for the attack, their lances were less effective against the wall of Roman shields on the higher ground. When the attack failed to break the Roman line, they retreated before the now-advancing Romans into a cadre of Marius's soldiers that were concealed and waiting at their rear.

The result was catastrophic. Over a hundred thousand Teutons died in the battle and another two or three hundred thousand were taken prisoner and either killed or sold into slavery. It was said that the Arc River ran red with blood and that the *vignerons* later took the bones to build fences for their vineyards. As an offering to Martha, his prophetess, Marius herded a number of Teutons to the top of the mountain named after his victory and had them thrown down an abyss known as the Garagaï. After the battle, he learned that he had been elected consul of Rome for a fourth time. He was to go on to be elected a staggering seven times in his lifetime.

The battle broke the strength of the barbarian tribes and fixed the course of history for the region. The Romans were firmly in control and could introduce their well-structured form of government. They didn't have a name for the region, so they simply referred it as a province of Rome—Provence.

Soon, a sign for Puyloubier and the D623 appeared, taking us west and away from the battleground. Instead, I saw the south flank of Ste-Victoire coming into view, with its sheer cliffs and the Cross of Provence glowing in the morning sun. A half-hour later we passed the raised terrain of the Barre du Cengle and entered the pine forests leading to the village of Le Tholonet.

"We're on the Route Cézanne," Hélène said. "Cézanne hiked in here and painted Ste-Victoire over eighty times, trying to capture its different moods. Do you remember his painting we saw in London? The one with the pine boughs blurred as they waved in the wind and the village painted in such sharp detail? This is it—Le Tholonet."

It was Sunday and the villagers had gathered at the *boule* courts in the shade of the trees. We stopped and watched the play for a while, listening to the clank of the balls and the cries of the players.

From Le Tholonet, Aix was a short drive through a pine forest and then the suburbs appeared. It was almost noon and we had come full circle and around the mountain and still had our picnic lunch untouched in our backpacks.

"Okay. Let's drive to the dam site for the reservoir that supplies water to Aix," I volunteered.

We found the sign and turned off onto a small road leading to Lac du Bimont and the dam.

In fact there were two dams as well as the ruins of a Roman dam and aqueduct built to bring water to Aix. The Zola dam was built in the 19th century by the father of Émile Zola (I had once thought the dam was called the Cézanne), and the far-larger Bimont dam built after the Second World War under the Marshall Plan.

We drove up the road, parked and walked over to the Bimont dam. On one side, the water of the reservoir was lapping high on the convex curve of the concrete wall; on the other side was a vertiginous drop into a steep gorge almost ninety metres below. A placard next to the dam informed us that the reservoir was capable of holding 39 million cubic metres of water exerting more force against the dam than the mind can easily comprehend.

For me, dams are ominous things. Possibly my fascination comes from my youth, when a small earthen dam burst, flooding hundreds of cottages at a summer resort. Since then, whenever I look at a dam I see a thin wall of concrete holding back a mass of pent-up energy that is just waiting for an earthquake or design failure to catastrophically unleash a wall of water into the countryside in its path.

In this case the dam is directly above the Arc Valley, the village of Le Tholonet and the city of Aix. Furthermore, it was built on the Mid-Durance tectonic fault; and when cracks were discovered in the concrete, the decision was made that protective action had to be taken, so a warning system of foghorns was put in place to alert the residents if the dam failed. On hearing the horns, the residents would immediately perceive the danger and have several minutes to hop in their cars and outrun the 39 million cubic metres of water hurtling down upon them at some incalculable speed.

"Let's find a spot above the dam for a picnic," Hélène said as we walked back to the car.

We picked up our backpacks and hiked into the trees until we reached a clearing beside the lake. Across the lake rose Mont Ste-Victoire. We stopped, feeling lazy and on our own. Or so we thought until we saw a young couple, unaware of us, sunbathing nude on the opposite shore.

Hélène spread a tablecloth on a flat rock while I uncorked the wine. The bottle, still wrapped in newspaper, was cool to the touch. We tore off bits of *baguette*, sliced the cheese and *charcuterie* and sipped rosé while lying back and relaxing in the warmth of the sun. The azure tone of the water reflected the pine-covered slope of the mountain behind. A breath of air stirred the water, causing the smooth surface to shimmer with sunlight. I thought about how Cézanne had painted the wind.

Having finished the bottle of wine with amazing ease, we couldn't help noticing that the sunbathers were becoming increasingly preoccupied. We packed our backpacks and slipped away.

Chapter 13
much ado about guests

CHARLES AND FERN were special to us, so it was arranged that they would be staying for a week. We had lodged this commitment in our minds as an event being some distance off until, one day in August, we realized that they were about to arrive.

"We should plan an itinerary," Hélène said as we worked together, preparing the garden suite.

I thought for a moment. "How about a drive around the hills of Les Dentelles de Montmirail?"

"Why there?"

"It's got everything. The Roman ruins in Vaison-la-Romaine are only twenty minutes from here. From there we can drive around Les Dentelles and wind up back at Vaison and be home in time for dinner. Think about it. There's that perched village of Le Crestet on the east side, then Malucene. We could even drive up Mont Ventoux.

Its peak has a stunning view—it's some 1,912 metres or 6,275 feet."

"How do you know *that*?"

"Biking. It's called the '*Géant de Provence*' for good reason. Every rider considers it one of the greatest cycling ascents. Only the elite riders try it. . . . Did you know that in midwinter the mistral has been recorded at 320 kilometres per hour, or 200 miles per hour?"

"Now you're showing off."

"No, just reading the local history, and—"

"And where do we go from there?"

"We could have lunch at Les Géraniums in Le Barroux at the south end of the hills. It has superb *provençale* food. Charles is an oenophile, so after that we could stop at Baumes-de-Venise where they make that Muscat dessert wine. From there we can start north again and do some wine tasting at Vacqueyras, Gigondas and even Sablet and Séguret if there's time. Séguret has that stunning view over the Rhône Valley. Then we are almost back at Vaison again and only minutes from here."

"Mhm," Hélène said while brushing a pool of cat fur from the duvet cover.

"I'll set out fresh towels and put up the curtains. There's not enough time to finish painting the walls. Okay, I like your plan," she added.

We had arranged to pick up our guests at the train station in Montélimar, which is about a half-hour drive from Nyons, so on the morning of their arrival we set off on the D538. Traffic was light, so we had arrived a bit early and took the opportunity to stroll along a pleasantly treed street and window-shop before entering the station to find a vacant bench and wait. At precisely the scheduled time, the high-speed train or *train à grande vitesse* (TGV), a model of efficiency, glided smoothly into the station, disgorged its passengers, took on new ones and departed. In a matter of moments it had accelerated into the distance.

The people who had disembarked were already making their way out of the station to waiting friends or family, but there was no sign of Charles and Fern. I walked the length of the platform and back and shrugged my shoulders. "I don't see them. Do we have the right train?"

Hélène looked at her notes. "This is the right time and train number. Fern gave me the information when she called last night."

At that moment, a loudspeaker blared. "Would *Monsieur* and *Madame* Bitney please come to the *gendarmerie.*"

We looked at each other, got up and located the office. A young *gendarme* was standing at the counter as we walked in the door and we identified ourselves to him.

"*Asseyez-vous, s'il vous plaît,*" he said stiffly. We found two chairs and sat down.

"This looks serious," Hélène said in a low voice. A few minutes passed and nothing more happened. She began to shift anxiously in her chair. "Wait here," she said as she got up and walked back to the counter.

"Pardon me, but is there anything wrong?" The *gendarme* looked up and must have seen the concern on her face for his brisk manner suddenly melted.

"I *am* sorry, *madame!* I should have explained. We have received a message that your friends missed their train. They have been rerouted and should arrive in three hours. Why don't you return then?"

My wife showed visible relief and thanked him.

We had seen the shops and it was almost noon, so we walked over to a *bistrot* a block away to pass the time over an extended French lunch and a *demi* of wine. Back at the station, the slower local train rumbled in with none of the aerodynamic grace of the TGV.

Charles appeared, bony and disjointed as an ostrich, his face thin, with a hooked nose on which his wire-framed glasses took their perch. He had earned 'Ostrich' as a nickname in his teens and it had stuck. His appearance happened to match well with his fine, but rather absorbed, legal mind.

"God, we're so glad to see you," Charles said as he towed two large pieces of luggage behind him. "I'd no idea if you'd get the message. I guess you did, did you?"

"We were told you missed your train and they gave us your new arrival time," I said, playing it down.

"Missed the train? We got on the *wrong* one."

We loaded the suitcases in the car and got underway. Charles seemed to have dropped the subject. However, once we were on the road heading out of Montélimar he began again.

"Fern and I made it to the train station at Charles de Gaulle airport and walked down to the platform with fifteen minutes to spare, so we sat down and waited. When the TGV pulled in we got on and found our seats. I don't know why, but I checked my watch and it was five minutes early. The TGV is *always* on time. *Gawd*, I knew immediately we were on the wrong bloody train—and it was already pulling out of the station."

"It wasn't real serious, Char," Fern interjected. Then, turning to us, "You have to understand from the get-go that Charles' mind is always off somewhere else than where it ought to be." She had clearly developed a way of shrugging off his errors yet leaving him seemingly in charge.

Charles continued, "I went and found the conductor and he got us off at the next stop, took us into the station and in minutes they had us rerouted on these slow local trains. Then I realized you'd be waiting so I asked them to have you paged at this station. We're beat. We've been doing planes and trains for over eighteen hours."

"Well, we're very glad you're here. The sun is shining and your room is ready," Hélène said, moving along to the next subject for the rest of the drive to Nyons.

After our guests were installed in the new suite and had had a chance to freshen up, they came into to the kitchen where we were preparing dinner.

"Well, that feels better. What can we do?" Charles offered.

Hélène took charge. "There's a bottle of champagne in the fridge, and glasses in the cupboard above. Do you want to open it and pour four glasses?"

"Champagne?"

"To your arrival!"

While I went on setting the table, I could see him removing the metal capsule and undoing the wire muzzle holding the cork in place. Then I heard a series of inarticulate sounds that escalating into grunting.

"This cork is really stuck." Charles now had the bottle in one hand and was muscling at the cork with his other hand. "It won't budge."

I left him to it and went on putting the cutlery on the table. A moment later I heard a loud 'pow' and turned to see Charles with his head held high, both hands gripping the neck of the champagne bottle and his two thumbs in the air where the cork had just been lodged. Champagne was bubbling over his hands.

"You've got it!" I said, reaching for the gushing bottle.

Charles was not moving and his mouth was open. A red mark was forming in the middle of his forehead.

"*Oooh,*" was all he said.

He let go of the bottle and touched his forehead.

"Ow," he added.

Fern came over. "*Hello?* What's happened? Are you alright, Char? Come over here and sit down so that I can take a *boo* at you," she said smoothly, taking charge of the situation. Charles obeyed as if he had had years of experience following her suggestions.

"It looks okay," she said, inspecting what was now a bright welt. "You've been lucky, dear. It could have hit you in the eye. Going forward it will be just fine. We'll put some ice on it."

During their stay with us, we wanted to try the tour of Les Dentelles that we'd planned, so we allowed for a day of rest and then got ready for the excursion the day after that. When it arrived, we all rose early. Charles came up the stairs wearing a crumpled Tilley safari hat that was pitched awkwardly on his head and a matching khaki shirt and shorts. I was pleased to see there was no oversized camera dangling from a strap around his neck. Fern followed behind him, dressed in a cotton blouse and bright-coloured shorts. She had a straw hat in one hand.

Charles and I got in the front seats of the car and Fern in the back, while Hélène opened the sagging old wood gate and, after I backed the car out, closed it again.

As I drove, my wife and Fern were in the back seat talking nonstop. Fern had just referred to the TGV as 'world-class' when Charles began saying something while continuing to stare at the road ahead; it seemed as if he wasn't so much talking as verbalizing what was going through his mind.

"Before we left Vancouver there was a story circulating around our firm about a case in the U.S. Apparently, a rather headstrong American tort attorney had bought several boxes of extravagantly expensive cigars. When he had smoked them all he then made a claim against his insurance company for fire loss. Of course the insurer denied the claim. So he sued them and actually won the case. In any event the worm turned, for after the case was over the insurer pressed charges for arson and the man was convicted; after all he had set fire to the insured cigars."

There was a moment of silence and then, in chorus from the back seat, "*Impossible!*" The conversation in the back returned to where it had left off. Charles wore an impish grin.

Vaison-la-Romaine is less than twenty minutes from Nyons and we spent most of the morning exploring the Roman ruins and then returned to the car to drive on to Crestet.

On passing a stone farmhouse with laundry hanging from a clothesline in the yard, Charles said, "That reminds me . . ." as if once again ruminating on something. I glanced at him to see his eyes once again fixed on the road ahead. "One morning last winter I had gone over to my club to play tennis. After we played, I was stripping down to shower when I saw one of the guys staring at me. He seemed embarrassed and then he just walked away. So I looked down and all I had on were these frilly ladies' panties."

Fern burst out giggling from the back seat of the car. "Yeah, we'd had a hot night and I wanted to remind him."

"But how—" was all I got out when Charles went on.

"I was stuck. I didn't have any jockey shorts with me, so I'd gone into one of the toilet stalls and put on the panties and then my tennis gear and went out and played."

"He's just *tooo* absent-minded," she said. "He forgot about the panties after playing." She was giggling again.

By then we had reached the perched village of Crestet and started to drive up the hill.

"Crestet is one of those stunning medieval villages," Hélène said, playing travel guide. "It's a must-see."

When we reached the hilltop, we parked the car to take in the view over the green hills of Buis-les-Baronnies, and walked the narrow cobbled lanes that wind along the steep hillside like goat trails between the old stone houses. Then, back in the car, we headed south for Le Barroux at the southernmost point of Les Dentelles and I could hear Fern telling Hélène about how wonderfully well Charles' practice in the arcane area of copyright law was going.

As it was approaching noon, we were easily on time to stop in Le Barroux at Les Géraniums Restaurant. Once seated, Charles was showing interest in the wine list. I knew he was keen on wines and asked him to order the wine while the rest of us looked over the lunch menu. We started with a white Châteauneuf-du-Pape to accompany the *salades* and then he gleefully selected a special vintage of red Gigondas for the *entrées* to follow. That was a lot of wine for lunch, but Charles wanted to try the local wines, '*in situ*' as he called it.

Hélène and Fern seemed to be taking a rest from their running conversation and, after we were well into the red,

I knew by the change in his voice that Charles was about to tell another story.

"You know," he opened, "last fall my wine club invited a wine writer to one of our dinners. It was an honour to have such a famous man in attendance. When everyone was arriving, he was already seated at a table with a pile of his latest book beside him, which he was ready to sell and sign. He did the signing in green ink with a great flourish of his Montblanc fountain pen.

"I hadn't organized the dinner, but I had gotten to know the head waiter, having organized past events at the restaurant. The man oversaw the wines with meticulous care. He worked hard to see that everything moved in a timely fashion. The waiters poured the wines at a sideboard and then carried the glasses to the tables to match the arrival of each food course. That was unusual, since wines are usually poured *at* the tables, but it allowed all the pours to be the same size. The wine writer rose frequently to talk about the wines. He spent a good deal of time talking about two wines in particular that were from adjacent vineyards that one *vigneron* owned, and the subtle differences to be found in the soil of plots that are just yards apart on the same hillside. He described what made each wine distinct from the other. His memory and knowledge was encyclopaedic. He said every year he would visit the vineyards, and the *vigneron* always smiled delightedly at him throughout the tastings. We all tasted the wines searching for the characteristics he described, following his every word. It was a *tour de force* performance.

"I could see that the head waiter was on edge the entire evening and even more so during the discussion of the wines, no doubt anxious to see that all went well with such an illustrious guest.

"Afterward, as we were getting up to leave the room, the head waiter came over to talk to me. I thought he was anxious for my approval and so I told him that the evening had been a great success.

"He accepted my praise very graciously and then said, 'But please, Mr. Stevens, I didn't want to tell you this while the great man was talking—the waiters mixed up the bottles.'"

Charles broke out in raucous laughter at this point. "*Some* connoisseur," he said, taking a great sip of the Gigondas in his glass. "The guy knew everything about the wines that there was to know—but he couldn't *taste* them!"

By 2:30 in the afternoon we were back on the road and heading toward Vacqueyras for a wine tasting at a *domaine* that I had mentioned to Charles earlier that morning. The problem was that by the time we had finished off two bottles of wine over lunch and a Beaume de Venice with dessert, a tasting was the last thing we needed. However, Charles was fully engaged and wasn't willing to pass up the opportunity, and so we stopped and tasted.

From Vacqueyras the next village to the north lies in the famed appellation of Gigondas. By this time the flow of conversation in the back seat had slowed. As for Charles, he must have considered the afternoon a once-in-a-lifetime chance to taste the local wines. He had found his toy store, so to speak. I was tasting and spitting out the wine, trying to remain sober. However, Charles was no longer just tasting the wines; he was drinking.

I tried to play down the wines of Sablet as we drove through, but he saw a farm with its '*dégustation*' sign in the driveway and insisted we stop. We did. And by the time we left there he was no longer interested in perched villages or history. He was looking for new places to stop.

I sped past the vineyards below Séguret and on toward Vaison-la-Romaine and home to Nyons. Our carefully planned guest tour had flowed, so to speak, in its own direction.

When we arrived at our house the old wood gate in the driveway was gone. In its place was the wrought-iron gate we had ordered in April. There was no invoice in the mailbox. The *ferronnier* who had made it for us would be in touch soon enough.

Chapter 14
the carnival of summer

I WAS NO LONGER riding just for the adventure of exploring the countryside. My attention had shifted to gauging the length and the time of each ride. Near Grignan a pack of riders passed me, all pedalling quickly and in perfect synchronicity. I picked up my speed and dropped in behind the last rider to take advantage of his slipstream. Even on my all-purpose bike, with my improved conditioning I was able to stay at their pace. I rode with them for half an hour and then let myself fall back and watch them ride on into the distance before I turned and retraced my path home.

At our gate, I took off my helmet and rolled the bike slowly up the driveway. It had felt good to push myself. This had to be the feeling any serious athlete looks for: the desire to stretch oneself in order to feel alive. It occurred to me that I had been doing just that sort of thing most of my career, and now I was doing it on a bicycle.

Standing on the gravel patio before going indoors, I could see the rooftops of Nyons and, across the valley, Mont Garde Grosse with its forested north slope partly shaded from the afternoon sun.

Only a Frenchman would want to cycle up that—just as only the very best riders take aim at the much higher Mont Ventoux, the Holy Grail for serious cyclists.

At that moment a green 2CV sped up the road and a hand waved casually out the window. It occurred to me that I had never seen Pierre Luc at any sort of exercise.

Hélène was busy in the kitchen, while I was already at my desk, when I heard a knock at the front door.

"Can you get that?" she hollered. It was not a question, so I went downstairs.

"Violette!" I said when I opened the door. She was standing on the sill holding a large sack in both hands.

"*Bonjour*, Gordon," she said, looking up at me with a shy smile.

She had grown since last year and become a smaller mirror image of her mother, with the same blonde hair falling straight to the shoulders and the same eyes that somehow echoed the sky.

"*Maman* asked me to give you these."

She held out the sack for me to take. "*Abricots,*" she said, now swaying slightly from side to side.

"*Pour nous?*" I asked, showing delight at what was obviously a gift.

She smiled back and then got down to business. "*Est-ce-que* Marie-Hélène *est ici?*"

"*Certainement. Entre, entre,*" I said, encouraging her to come in.

"Hélène," I called out loudly. "Violette *est ici.*"

We climbed the staircase and walked into the kitchen where my wife was clipping leaves from the potted basil.

"*Regarde,*" I said, handing her the sack. "Violette brought us apricots."

Hélène broke into an explosion of thanks that clearly delighted Violette.

Then the two of them launched into a conversation in French that was too quick for me to follow. A few words were clear, like *très bleu*, which made Violette's blue eyes sparkle even more, and the word *chocolat* as Hélène reached into the cupboard for a box of chocolates. Next she brought out a carton of milk and glasses. I was beginning to feel like an interloper at Alice in Wonderland's tea party, so I excused myself and returned to my desk.

The fly was back as well, walking about between the letters on the screen, distracting me once more. Instead of settling back to work, I sat and thought about Violette's father. Pierre Luc had everything going for him. He owned a farm and had a beautiful wife and daughter, yet he seemed incapable of work. I shut off the computer and went outside in the warm sun and began laying out the tiles for the top of the wrought-iron coffee table.

That evening over dinner, Hélène told me that she had walked Violette home and talked to her mother.

"Fanny's worried," Hélène told me. "Although Pierre Luc doesn't hang out with his old buddies at the bar any more, he isn't doing all that's needed in a vineyard. She knows this from the courses on oenology that she took. He just doesn't seem to make the transition from talking to actually working. She doesn't understand why. She says he's a good man, but

143

he avoids doing what needs to be done. He should be going through the vineyard pinching off new growth and thinning the grape clusters. Fortunately the summer has been perfect for the grapes so far."

"Maybe he doesn't know how to work—he's never done it."

"Possibly."

"And so . . . ?"

"That's the question," she said as she walked over to the oven.

Hélène returned wearing an oven mitt and holding a torte made from Violette's apricots. She put both down on the table in front of me.

Using the mitt, I lifted the torte to my nose to sniff it, brushing the hot crust accidentally with my fingers. I set it back down and licked my fingers while Hélène cut pieces for us.

Not long after Violette's visit, apricots began to appear in the market, and Suzette called Hélène to ask if she would like to come over so they could make jellies together. When she accepted, I felt a pang of anticipation somewhere inside.

*   *   *

It was difficult to find a part of Provence that was *terra incognita*, as most every corner had been explored, vacationed in or purchased as a second home by foreigners. Yet the people of Provence remain largely unaffected and apart from these activities—perhaps for good reasons. After all, the English expatriates remained clannish and stuck together; the Dutch brought their own food with them; the Germans remained aloof; the Parisians were only there *en saison* to socialize around their swimming pools with Parisian friends. The locals referred to these people as either *les autres*—the others—or *les étrangers*—the strangers.

Also, with summer, new activities sprang to life, changing the otherwise tranquil villages and country roads. Driving west from Nyons to Vinsobres, we passed a recreational park with small wood cabins, tents and trailers all aligned in perfect military rows next to swimming pools brimming with splashing, squealing, giggling children. Like flocks of migratory birds, the vacationers had arrived—busy, noisy and curious. The annual summer flight to the sun was underway, and the villages and countryside had become one big moveable party.

The weekly markets swarmed with people who came to see a country market in action. Cars arrived to circle the village, creating bottlenecks, or *bouchons*, as the drivers sought parking that had long since disappeared. Disappointed, they parked illegally and returned to find their cars had been towed by the extra-vigilant *gendarmes*, who had found an easy bylaw to enforce.

The outdoor market of Nyons had expanded far beyond its normal size. Transformed into a bazaar—a festival of stalls—the market choked the squares and spread outward on the narrow streets like the straining tentacles of a restless creature that had temporarily taken over the village. Moving about in the milling crowds became increasingly difficult; bodies pressed together, rubbing shoulders and other body parts as people squeezed to pass one another. The atmosphere fed on itself, drawing even more people to see what the activity was all about.

The merchants rose to the invasion (good money was to be made in the few summer months) by targeting those who wanted something to show off back home, something *provençal*. Souvenirs such as pottery, olive-wood kitchen utensils, straw baskets and hats of various colours, antiques, clay cicadas, vividly-coloured *provençal* fabrics and mounds of rustic-looking sachets all artfully labelled '*Herbes de Provence*' could make a perfect gift for some friend or relative. The locals, in their turn, had to adjust to this influx by arriving earlier in the morning to do their shopping before the tourists were up and about.

The food stalls reach full bloom, with tables stacked high with fresh produce, inviting everyone to share in the feast from nearby farms: great piles of green heads of lettuce and red tomatoes and onions with their parchment skin, tangled heaps of yellow beans, green cucumbers aligned in rows, coral carrots and red radishes plucked from the earth and tied in bunches at their greens. The fruit stalls have their own look: baskets of ripe apricots, dark cherries and strawberries. All this fecundity of food forms an amazing array of garden colours.

Nor are the olfactory senses left out. Cauldrons of paella bubble next to chickens slowly turning on their spits, which are next to glistening fish on beds of ice. There are tables of jute sacks brimming over with spices and herbs, each with its wooden ladle inviting you to fill a bag or two. Then there are the leather goods still smelling from their tanning, the perfumed floral bouquets of the flower merchants, and straw *panniers* piled on the pavement in the sun hinting of their origins as dried grass in the fields. At a summer market, no nose escapes untantalized and no stomach goes unheard.

146

We needed a new *pannier* for our grocery runs, so Hélène stopped and began looking over the selection. Then the vendor appeared beside her. For what purpose was it to be used? What size? Colour? After some discussion, Hélène bought one with leather handles.

We had agreed to go our separate ways and meet up at noon at the Belle Epoque, so I left my wife looking at a white denim jacket on a rack of clothing. I walked about, passing a table with the harsh smell of *savons de Marseille* that pricked my nose. I continued somewhat aimlessly, wandering until a man caught my attention by waving something in his hand.

"*Un sac d'énergie!*" he hollered, looking at me. He had a sausage in one hand and a French Lagioule knife in the other.

He saw me hesitate and took advantage by lopping off a round with his Lagioule and holding it out for me to take.

For a moment I wondered what he was talking about, and then I caught on—he'd found his sales pitch by equating his sausages to an energy bar. After all, an energy bar and a sausage are both heavy in protein, both come sealed in their own package and both are easy to carry—just put it in a pocket or stuff it in a sack. Neither had to be warmed or prepared. All that was required was a knife to slice and eat a round of sausage whenever a pang of hunger took hold.

"*Mangez—essayez!*"—Eat it, try it! he commanded.

It was too late to say no. I took the round and bit off a corner.

"*Chèvre*"—goat, he said, as he quickly lopped a round off another sausage and held it out. "*Essayez celle-ci!*"

It was drier and chewier, with a richer, darker flavour than the first.

147

"*De Corse. Ça c'est cher, mais très bon,*" he added, saying it was very expensive.

"*Et celle-là.*" Already he was eagerly cutting more pieces. Clearly he wasn't going to let me get away until he found one I liked.

I stopped at a cheese stall and looked at the pungent camembert from the north of France that was oozing out of shape in the warm sun. Then I saw a Cavaillon melon. It was cut in half and placed in the middle of the merchant's cheeses. Taking a closer look, I noticed there was something different about it. It was the same size as a melon, with the same wrinkled grey rind, but the core was pitted and a darker orange than usual. I also didn't see any seeds. The merchant saw me looking at it.

"*C'est un* Mimolette," he said, cutting off a sliver and handing to me. "*Très vieux*"—very old, he added.

I had expected the honey taste of a moist Cavaillon melon. Instead it was a hard, tangy cheese with a long, nutty aftertaste. I agreed to buy a small wedge.

While wrapping it for me, he kept on talking. "You will enjoy this cheese. The little holes are nothing—just cheese mites. They're gone now." He handed me the package.

As I walked away, my attention was drawn to a tall man the colour of dark chocolate wearing a multi-coloured *kaftan* that draped his body completely and even wrapped around his head. Amid the bland dress of the crowd, all he needed to do was stand still, as he did, to attract attention. The *kaftan* gave such an overpowering sense of African authenticity that people were stopping, first to look at him and then to look over the leather goods he was selling. As I stood watching this little drama, he happened to glance my way and our eyes held for an instant. That was all it took for me to recognize him.

He was the waiter from the restaurant just down the street—only there he wore jeans and a T-shirt. Now he looked as if he had arrived straight from the hinterlands of Africa. He was busy selling merchandise, bowing graciously to answer questions, limiting his otherwise good French to a few stilted words. His voice had taken on a timbre that I hadn't heard before. He glanced my way a second time and smiled.

Mopeds buzzed the busy streets like oversized wasps in brash packs of two or three, weaving and darting around cars and people, causing pedestrians to jump back and then look cautiously before stepping out again. The harsh rasp of their unmuffled engines could be heard long before they appeared, ridden by teenagers who obviously loved the racket. The streets were crowded with shoppers, traffic was at a standstill and everyone seemed to be enjoying a good day. In the distance the mopeds could be heard dashing back and forth on the back streets until two riders appeared in the square, racing their engines and pushing forward, trying to force their way through the crowds of shoppers by dint of noise and intimidation. And then it happened.

One of the riders lost control of his moped and bumped a pedestrian—not hard enough to injure, and it might not have mattered too much—a small matter, really—but a *gendarme* happened to be standing there. He took a few steps, stopped in front of the two mopeds and raised his hand. Then he reached over the handle bars of one moped, shut the engine off and waited for the other rider to do the same. Rising to his full bureaucratic authority, he said something loudly and abruptly. The helmets that offered anonymity came off, revealing the faces of two boys, whose macho behaviour had all too rapidly dissolved.

149

A circle of observers had widened around the scene, as if taking in an impromptu circus act. When the *gendarme* finished and turned to walk away, someone began to clap softly, and then the clapping spread like a small breeze through the crowd. This was too much for the boys. Not daring to start their mopeds, helmets in hand, they chose to push them away. They were not seen or heard again.

La Belle Epoque was crowded. I saw our drywall installer there with his wife, the mayor at a table on his own, tradesmen lunching with their co-workers, as well as the usual mix of summer tourists. I looked around for Hélène and saw Alice instead.

"Have you seen Hélène?" I asked.

"Yes, she was here a few minutes ago looking for you, and she's gone off to buy bread. Sit down. I've held a table for you."

A few minutes later Hélène emerged out of the crowd. "This place is crazy today. I've never seen it so busy. You're having beer! Maybe I will too," she said as she sat down.

The new pannier was overflowing with produce, fresh flowers, a baguette and several plastic shopping bags.

"I bought that denim jacket, and I found the nicest lady selling sandals, so I got a pair. What did you do?"

"Oh, not too much—I found some sausages and cheese."

I reached down beside my chair for the bag to find a dog, straining on a leash from the next table, sniffing at it. I picked it up and handed it to her.

She saw the sausages inside. "*Ugh.* Well, I hope *you* enjoy them."

By the time we had finished lunch the market had closed, the merchants had gone and the crowds too. Civic street cleaners were picking up the last evidence of what had filled the squares and streets that Thursday morning.

•   •   •

Over the spring and early summer I had spent more time with Pierre Luc, learning about vineyards and grape-growing. One day he showed me the new spring growth of canes. A month later we walked the rows of vines together, with him on one side and me on the other, as he demonstrated how to prune back the leaves to expose the swelling clusters of grapes to the sun. Pierre Luc talked volumes, and I was happy to learn the French lexicon of vineyards.

The grape bunches, half hidden in the leafy foliage, are called *grappes*, while the individual grapes are *raisins*. *Taille* means the pruning of the vines. *Débourrement* or budbreak is when the new leaves first unfurl in the early spring. *Floraison* is the flowering. *Effeuillage* is the thinning of the leaves in June to expose the grape clusters to sunlight and promote their growth. *Véraison* indicates the grapes are beginning to turn colour and ripen in the summer. (Pierre Luc's Viognier grapes were turning from green to yellow with brown flecks over the skin.) *Mûrissant* is the actual ripening. Finally, once the grapes have fully ripened and reached optimal sugar content, *vendange* or harvest takes place. *Millésime* means the vintage.

There were risks, as I had seen the previous summer when a hailstorm wiped out part of a nearby vineyard. Rain was the great spoiler if it came too near the harvest.

151

To make the best wine the vines need tending throughout the summer, right up to the optimal moment to pick. Rain had to come at a time when it would stimulate growth, followed by hot sun to ripen the grapes. If the rain came just before or during the harvest, this was a disaster—the grapes would absorb the moisture, the concentration of sugar would be diluted and the wine would be insipid.

It is the right concentration of sugar that makes good wine. If the grapes are picked too early, the acidity might be too high.

These were the yardsticks for the *vigneron* as he watched the weather and the progress of his vineyard through a growing season. The hope and aspiration was that by fall it would all come together in a successful harvest and an outstanding vintage. Since no two growing seasons were exactly the same, each vintage produces unique and different wines.

Pierre Luc was happy to describe in detail the work that he should be doing. He admitted that many of the words he knew came from Fanny's university courses on wine-making. And he had his own vocabulary as well, for he talked in terms of the *death* of autumn, the *sleep* of winter, the *rebirth* of spring and the *growth* of summer. He said his father, like all good *vignerons*, measured time in vintages, not years.

I learned other words from him as well. A guy is a *mec*, a *copain* is a buddy, while *mon pote* is one's very best friend; breasts are *gros lolos*. One day he looked at a pretty girl and said "*Un beau châssis!*" That spoke for itself. I heard him refer to someone as *sympa* and later learned that meant the person was pleasant or sympathetic.

Another time he looked at his wife who was bending over weeding in the vegetable garden and said, *"Mon chou est adorable."*

"I thought *chou* was a cabbage, so why did he say it was adorable?" I asked Hélène later.

She smiled. "He doesn't have any cabbages! That's his wife."

"He calls her a cabbage?"

"Yes. *'Mon chou'* means his cabbage, all right, but it's colloquial for *'my sweetheart'!"*

∙   ∙   ∙

It was July and the Tour de France was underway. Nearly 200 riders had started out to cycle 3,500 kilometres (over 2,100 miles) around France in twenty days. There was something numbing about that. Every kilometre of the Tour is telecast live from helicopters hovering overhead to spectators around the world. This is far and away *the* most prestigious event in cycling, and fans can watch it—narrated by former greats of the sport—while taking in panoramic views of France's mountains, vast plains and fabulous *châteaux* from the comfort of their homes in front of their televisions.

With the American Lance Armstrong wearing the front-runner's yellow jersey, the Tour had an electrifying appeal. Even the French admitted to his prowess and treated him as one of their own.

Drawn by the spectacular coverage, we began spending more and more time indoors watching on our small TV. At first we thought that a cycling race spread over twenty days couldn't possibly hold our attention when the weather was sunny and warm outdoors. But this was the Tour de France—

the most gruelling cycling event on the planet.

One rainy day a rider lost traction in a corner and slid over the wet pavement hard into the metal barrier at the side of the road. Another day a competitor missed a turn on a mountain descent and crashed into a low stone wall, sending him over the top and down a rocky ravine. He survived, and the well-informed commentator reminded us that in 1935 in similar circumstances, someone had died.

I watched a cyclist at the front of the pack fall and take down dozens behind him, bringing the entire *peloton* to a screeching stop in a tangled heap of bent metal, skinned elbows and knees, and a few broken bones. The commentator made light of the situation by simply saying that these determined competitors were known to ride with broken wrists or collarbones—accidents were expected, pain could be endured, the race would go on.

I had learned that this summer's Tour was coming through our village. The stage that day was to begin at Vaison-la-Romaine, so the *peloton* would pass through Nyons in the morning and then continue into the Alps. This had to be even better than watching on television.

When we got there a crowd was already waiting at the side of the road and the local police were busy doing crowd control, though not much was happening. Soon a few cars and vans bearing logos of bicycle and clothing manufacturers drove by. Then once again nothing happened. A few media vehicles sped by. Next came the team vans carrying spare parts and bikes on roof racks. They were followed by two *gendarmes* on motorcycles.

The racers couldn't be far behind now, could they?

Several helicopters appeared over the hilltop and soared down metres over our heads, their blades whacking deafeningly, and just as quickly they were gone behind another hill. Then, without any fanfare, with a whizzing of gears and hissing of tires the first group of the *peloton* appeared, followed almost immediately by the main pack. I raised my camera, looked through the viewfinder and waited. Then there he was—Lance Armstrong wearing the yellow jersey as leader of the race. I snapped the picture.

By the time I had lowered the camera the riders had passed and were rounding a far bend in the road. I watched a few laggards struggling at the rear, and then they were gone as well. The spectators were already dissolving into just a milling crowd of people; the police were pulling back the barricades. We had seen the Tour de France.

When we reached home and turned on the TV, the race was already into the mountains. Once again the panoramic vistas of the countryside from the helicopters high overhead and the shots of the riders on the roads below held our attention. As always, the Tour would end with tens of thousands of spectators lining Avenue des Champs-Élysées in Paris.

Chapter 15
scents of summer & Saharan dust

IN ARLES WE HAD SEEN glossy, green jasmine that ran up the wall and over the entrance to a restaurant. As we passed through the mantle, it gave off an enchantingly intense, spiced honey scent. We took a cutting away with us and showed it to our nursery owner when we returned to Nyons, asking if she could find the same variety. She smiled and led us into the yard of the nursery where she pointed out several tubs. We bought copious amounts and planted it along the east side of our house below the bedroom window.

It took us a while to learn that jasmine is a demanding plant, requiring an abundance of water to grow and thrive in the summer heat. We gave it the water, and it rewarded us the first year with steady growth and then the second year with a stellar flowering of tiny white blossoms and heady fragrance. A little reading revealed that there were many species of jasmine. In Indonesia it is used in wedding ceremonies; in Thailand it represents the mother; in Damascus it is the symbol of the city; it is also associated with life, seduction and procreation. The word derives from the Persian *yasameen*, meaning 'gift from God.' It can also be a night-blooming flower.

This year, when the spring rapidly gave way to summer, we waited for the blossoms to return once more. And when they did and the heat of the sun had done its work, the blossoms opened at dusk and the fragrance wafted in the open windows to where we slept. It would stay the night with us and then wane with the morning; it lasted through the long weeks of summer.

•   •   •

I was not listening to music, I was riding my bike—its cadence was enough for me. This was my time to be alone and leave my mind free to raise any thoughts it wanted to—a sort of stream of consciousness with no rules, more like meditating—on a bike, of all places. Thoughts appeared, like the puffy clouds that arrived overhead, and then faded away, leaving just the more solid ones for further reflection. I did not get on a bike to problem-solve or anything as rigorous as that. However, riding had become a place I was happy with, away from garden work or other jobs that required my attention. I tend to think in a discursive manner, that is to say, rambling and jumping from one thing to another, then fitting the thoughts together into a more rational whole. It's not a logical progression at all. Occasionally two ideas come together to form a new thought or a conclusion. Intuition must work like this.

157

As I rode today, one of the fighter jets from the military base near Orange flew low overhead, ripping the sky apart with its shrieking sound. It happened so quickly I barely had time to look up before its black shadow was already passing out of sight. This brought my thoughts back to the road ahead, and I calculated the distance to the next village.

I had come to know these hills well, for I had spent two seasons now riding the roads and trails. I knew the farms and had watched them change through the spring and summer. I also realized that I had changed as well.

Sometimes I chose a one-lane track in order to get closer to some stone building, such as the old *mas* in the distance (built from stones dug out of these fields generations ago), now occupied by a farmer whose children were playing outdoors.

Once, a dog tore out from another farmyard, barking and dashing at me. It was a huge brute and seemed intent on attack. I was lucky—by standing up on the pedals and pumping hard I successfully outdistanced it. I had heard of deer attacking motorcycles and bicycles. Maybe this was the same instinct at work.

My all-purpose bike was great on rough gravel and dirt; it was not a road bike with narrow tires built for speed—that was not what I rode for. At first it was for exercise, and then an exploration of the countryside. And then it became a place for me to think about the things that were on my mind.

●   ●   ●

In the hot, dry climate of late summer the sun-baked vineyards became pregnant and heavy with clusters of grapes that hung below the leaves. When I spent time in the garden

I wore a hat for protection from the sun. Working one day in the intense heat, my mind wandered back to cooler times when we had travelled in France . . . . Earlier in the spring we had stopped beside the Loiret River in the Loire Valley for lunch at Les Quatre Saisons Restaurant with its covered veranda that had once been a boathouse. We had been seated next to the railing, looking across to the far treed shore where elegant white boathouses reached out into the water. The restaurant was tranquil as the tourist season had not kicked in yet, so we pretty well had the place to ourselves. We decided to indulge ourselves, so we shared a dish of *cuisses de grenouilles en persillade*—frogs legs with a parsley and garlic sauce that the waiter put between us, and we ate with our fingers. For a main course I had *truite au fenouil et au citron*—baked trout with fennel, shallots and lemon that had been added to the menu for the day. Hélène had *salmon aux herbes*—salmon with herbs. The chilled Chablis was clean and crisp. A light shower swept through, the drops dancing on the surface of the river . . . .

As the reverie faded, dripping with perspiration, T-shirt stuck to my back, I surveyed my garden work. The outdoor shower half-concealed in the trees was getting steady use. Tabitha and Myrtille had stretched out on a concrete pad in the full sun, unmoving, as if deaf to the waves of the cicadas' mounting song to the hot weather.

The cerulean sky was becoming dull, as if a dome of tinted glass were being lowered in place overhead. The air was unusually calm and heavy. Furthermore, a fine ochre dust had settled on the garden furniture and all the other surfaces as well: the tiled balcony, the leaves on the trees and the car. When François came by that afternoon, I asked him about this curious phenomenon.

159

"It's the sirocco, a hot wind that blows from North Africa. That's from a sandstorm in the Sahara Desert. The dust travels on the prevailing winds across the Mediterranean."

Over the next few days the dust continued to settle on everything and even penetrated inside the house. It was the same colour as the *provençal* soil, and I wondered how many eons this transfer of fine powder had been going on and whether Provence wasn't in fact some sort of extension of the Sahara Desert.

On the fourth day of the sirocco, working in the garden, even in the shade of the trees, became increasingly difficult. When the sun rose toward noon, the heat was so intense I stopped to rest and drink water. It gave me an excuse to stand up and look at the progress I had made and gauge what more there was to do. I no longer seemed to hear the cicadas so much as feel their brash noise like a physical irritant. I found Myrtille napping in the deep shade of the garden, where she had smoothed a small circle in the loose soil. She raised her head to look at me as I passed and then went back to sleep.

I had slowed in my work, even though the weeding had gone well and I had cleared an area that had been a problem for some time. I had been using a garden fork to loosen the weeds and extract the roots. Straightening up again, I pushed the fork into the ground and leaned on it. I had a another sip of water and then grabbed the fork. It stuck there. I gave it a harder tug, and it came out of the ground along with a section of plastic tubing that was dripping water. I let out a low groan, for I had just put the fork through the underground watering system.

I walked up to the house to shut off the water, then repaired the puncture and reburied the tube. Walking about in the sun

160

was no longer pleasant; it felt more and more like I was labouring in a hot forge. Hélène came out to see how the work was going, looked at my progress and went back indoors to make lunch.

It was not long before I heard her call, "*Déjeuner— à table!*"

When I had washed up and arrived in the kitchen, the awning was already extended over the balcony where Hélène was setting the table.

"Could you pour me some more wine?"

I saw her almost-empty glass of red wine on the table and a bottle next to it, so I refilled the glass. It turned pale pink. I had accidentally poured a white wine.

"Oh, you've opened a rosé. That's nice," she said as she carried out a *salade de chèvre chaude*, a warm goat cheese salad, and placed it on the table.

I sat down and looked out over the village and across the valley at Garde Grosse and saw a green 2CV driving up the road. Fanny and Violette were returning home for lunch. Moments later, the new neighbour just up the hill who ran a computer store in the village followed on his motorcycle. He and his wife had had a new baby over the winter. Every now and then, when the air was still, we could hear the baby crying. It was noon and everyone was heading to a place that was shaded from the sun for a lengthy lunch. I stood on the balcony, tasting the wine, and felt the heat radiating through the awning over our heads. Without it the balcony would have been unusable in midday.

"I never did get together with Alice," Hélène said, sitting down. "So I stopped at the Belle Epoque for coffee. We had a long chat. Her daughter is now five years old. They live above the boutique she ran in the building her parents own.

She's not keen on working at the restaurant, yet the money is reliable compared to running her boutique which was only seasonal."

We ate and talked, had another glass of wine and leaned back in our chairs for a while longer. Finally, we rose to clean up the dishes.

I had found conversation difficult and returned to the heat of the garden with the thought I would do more weeding. Instead, I was unusually lethargic. The sun overhead felt heavy and black. I bent over to pick up my gloves and immediately knew it was a mistake, for in that full sun a dull ache and dizziness overcame me and my eyes lost focus. Something was wrong. I pulled myself up and sat down on the garden wall, lowered my head between my knees and remained there for several minutes. A sense of relief followed, but when I raised my head again, the ground turned beneath me. I slowly stood up and went indoors. I hadn't been in the sun all that long, I thought—how could this have happened?

When I entered the kitchen Hélène looked at me strangely. "Are you okay?"

I didn't answer.

She walked over to the sink and poured a glass of water. "Here, drink this."

I did.

"Sit down."

I did.

"You're having a shower." She led me into the bathroom and turned on the shower taps. "Take off your clothes and get in."

The water was cool and soothing. I just stood there, head under the running water, leaning against the wall.

I awoke in bed later. It felt luxurious, but my head ached; it felt as if there was a large stone loose inside.

"Feeling better?" Hélène asked, coming in with a glass of water. "You've had heatstroke."

I drank the water and fell asleep again. When I awoke, Hélène had made a salad. I ate sparingly, not feeling hungry.

The following day I was so sensitive to the sun I was unable to step outdoors. When I did, loud alarm bells rang in my head. The next day I was improving, and by the third day I was feeling considerably better.

I had watched François work in the direct sun for hours, only walking over to the outdoor shower and dousing his head from time to time before returning to work.

While I rested, Hélène began spending long hours with Suzette, returning home with jars of freshly-made jams still warm from their preparation.

"It reminds me of growing up in Quebec with my mother cooking over a wood-burning stove," she said. "Life revolved around that stove and the kitchen. It was the centre of our household activities. The family gathered there, talked, ate, washed up the dishes after dinner and played games at the same table."

As she talked I could feel her enthusiasm.

"French kitchens are small but are still the centre of activity. Suzette buys overly ripe fruit that the farmers almost give away because they don't think it will last another day. She doesn't use sugar. The apricots are so ripe and full of nectar they're dripping juice. I could almost taste them just from their aroma. We'll make *pâte de coing* in the fall."

"What's that?"

"A thick quince paste. Oh, and we're going to make some quince jelly too."

* * *

Perhaps as a result of my convalescence, one morning I awoke from a dream of cycling on a mountain. As I became more fully awake I found that it hadn't faded away, as most dreams do. At first it seemed like a farrago of disconnected elements. What did my cycling have to do with a mountain?

It stayed in the back of my mind, but began to grow as the day went on. *Cycle up a mountain such as Mont Garde Grosse?* It could be a good extension of my rides so far, and it would test my conditioning. The mountain was close by, only minutes away from our house. We had driven to the peak to take in the view, so I knew the road well. Then I realized that the decision had already been made before I was fully awake that morning. I pulled out my maps and began to calculate the ride.

When I rode into the village the following morning, I studied the flank of Garde Grosse with the road zigzagging upward through the forest toward the telecommunications tower at the peak. The summit is 944 metres above sea level and almost 700 metres above the valley floor of Nyons.

I had been riding a bike for less than four months and I was about to try climbing a mountain.

Chapter 16

*how to wreck your sex life ~ an ascent
and a quick descent*

To have loved, to have thought, to have done . . .

THE WEATHER REMAINED hot for another week and had taken
ownership of all our activities. We dashed between pockets of
shade. The car, if left in the sun, heated to furnace temperatures
within minutes. The air remained heavy, and Saharan dust
still covered every surface. By contrast, most nights were a
pleasant respite. Once the sun had set, we opened the shutters
and windows that had been closed all day to keep the heat out
and let in the cooler and more fragrant air.

Today it remained hot well after dark, so, seeking a cooler
space, we decided to move to the garden suite downstairs.
Just the same, by midnight, even with the sheets thrown off
the bed, it was still difficult to sleep.

I rose and walked over to the French doors that were already opened to the patio and stood on the sill wearing just boxer shorts. My wife came to stand beside me. We remained there without speaking for several minutes. In the utter calm of the night air, we could hear a door close somewhere in the village below.

"I'm going to have a shower," I said.

"I will too," she replied, and followed me across the gravel patio.

A broad band of stars traversed the sky from north to south; the night shadows of the garden lay black and impenetrable. The shower enclosure with its bamboo siding and six-sided canvas tent-top was situated well away from the house, in a secluded corner under the trees. The overhead nozzle was fifteen inches in diameter so that the water fell like rain, first warm from the section of the pipe that was above ground and then cold. It was operated by pulling a chain that released the water for thirty seconds and then automatically shut off. It took surprisingly long to feel the cool water penetrate the body and provide relief from the heat of the day, so I pulled the chain repeatedly. We stood near each other with our faces turned upward to catch the cascading water, letting it wash back our hair and run down our bodies, staying until we finally felt cool. Then we towelled down and walked barefoot over the coarse gravel and back indoors, where the soft, dry sheets of the bed welcomed us.

Later, awaking to the familiar sound of the church bell tolling in the village, I raised myself up on one elbow. The moon had risen and cast a beam of silver light that stretched across the patio onto the tiled floor next to our bed. There was a leisurely sense of movement in the air. The shadow of a cat moved across the doorway and disappeared into the garden. A minute later the church bell repeated its distant toll.

I awoke once more to hear birds cheeping—the precursor of dawn. I had already decided this was the day to cycle up Mont Garde Grosse.

And so my small saga began . . . . I slide quietly from the bed, put on my cycling gear and roll my bike out of the garage and over to the gate, closing it gently behind me. This ride has to be done before the sun can deliver its anvil blow to the day ahead. The night sky is deep indigo, perforated by only a few of the brighter stars. By the time I have coasted down the hill and begun pedalling across the small bridge at the foot of our hill, the eastern horizon is already lightening. I wonder for a moment if I am taking on too big a challenge, so I concentrate on pedalling to dismiss the thought.

The streets of the village are empty and silent. I see only one car moving and wonder where the driver could be going at this hour. Then I reach the village square, cross the bridge over the Aygues River and ride through a tunnel cut through a rock outcrop that forms the very foot of Garde Grosse.

When I come out the other side, the sun is already on the tips of the nearby peaks and the sky has a robin's-egg glow. Within a hundred yards I swing to the right onto a narrow road that angles upward onto the mountain and the climb begins. Immediately I feel the change of gradient and the increased effort it demands. Here, I enter a small valley that traverses one side of the mountain and ride steadily past houses on the rising slope. At first it is populated by houses, but those are soon replaced by farms.

Finally, the hamlet of St-Rimbert appears. Here, at the upper end of the valley where it peters out, the terrain opens onto a stretch of farmland, giving me some relief from the unrelenting strain of pedalling uphill. The road angles across the last bit of level ground and then at a sharp turn suddenly the incline is more demanding and the real ascent begins. A road up a mountain requires switchbacks, and now the road begins its zigzag pattern back and forth, turning the face of the mountain into a series of stages. Having driven to the top, I know that from this point on there will be no more level ground to rest until I reach the summit.

Gearing down, I bend over the handlebars, leaning into the more strenuous work, pumping harder on the pedals. The effort I am putting out actually feels good, telling me my conditioning is sound and I am ready for the climb. All the same, it doesn't take long for me to feel my quads tightening into steel bands. More straight stretches and turns until I am high enough to see over the ridge of the valley to Nyons far below.

The next turn takes me around to the other side of the mountain; the view of Nyons is gone. The constant uphill effort is burning in my legs. Yet, if I stop to rest I may have trouble starting again, so instead I ease my pace slightly to conserve energy for the remaining stages of the climb—this is a learning experience in managing my resources.

My breathing becomes dry, shallow gasps as my lungs press hard against my ribs. My leg muscles, growing increasingly taut, seek escape from every pedal stroke; they have become alien complainers, no longer my own. My knees feel as if they will explode. The next switchback in the road is steeper and sharper than the earlier ones and, rounding it, I suddenly realize I have lost momentum and am close to toppling sideways.

I quickly drop down a gear and stand up on the pedals to overcome the sudden demand. The bike saws from side to side and then, in the middle of the turn with my full weight on it, one pedal gives way beneath me and everything very quickly comes undone. My foot slides from the pedal and I drop like a stone, hitting the crossbar hard, bone on metal. The next moment I am lying on one side in the low gravel apex of the corner. Pain can reach such numbing intensity that the brain overrides, cancelling its effects, and I am in that zone. At first I can't move. The bike is on top of me. I am winded by the fall and my right arm is pinned under me. I lie there, gasping for breath, until slowly a shallow rhythm returns.

Finally, with my upper free leg I push the bike away and roll over onto my hands and knees with my head near the ground. Straightening up is difficult. First, I feel my arm for breaks and find none. I have scrapes from shoulder to ankle, but I seem to still be a male despite my encounter with the crossbar. Pulling the water bottle off the holder, I limp over to a rock and sit there without moving, feeling the early morning sun on my back. It must be fifteen or twenty minutes before I stand up to look at the bike.

The chain had pulled off the gears, causing the pedals to spin free and the bike to fall. It is undamaged. All I have to do is lift the rear wheel, turn the pedals and align the chain to spin it back onto the sprockets. I am the one with the damage. I know I will stiffen up later, but for now I can probably continue the ride.

Getting back on the bike is a tender operation. I am careful not to sit on the saddle while pedalling and begin gingerly in the lowest gear, avoiding any unnecessary exertion. Somehow riding relieves the pain, though the fall has taken its toll.

Finally, as the road straightens once more, I see ahead the open ground of the mountaintop and realize that all the switchbacks are behind me. This is the last hundred metres—the climb is now within my reach and I find a renewed energy to cover the remaining distance.

Emerging from the trees and rolling to a stop, I have arrived at the peak in the morning sun next to the France Telecom tower. The mountain drops away on all sides—I overlook an entire uninterrupted countryside. Standing, straddling the bike, I take time to gaze in all directions, and become aware of my breathing and heartbeat settling back to normal. From this height there is a pristine calm to the morning air, as if the land itself is not yet awake. *The ride was not so bad*, I think, now that it is finished.

Far below, Nyons lies nestled in its valley beside the Aygues River amid vineyards and orchards of fruit and olive trees. By tracing the roads and the river, I can just make out our house on the side of a hill bathed in sunlight. From here, the whole world seems stretched out below, level and benign, the nearby hills flattened in comparison to the greater elevation where I am standing. The familiar roads we drive are mere pencil lines in the landscape. The Rhône Valley in the distance remains half lost in the morning mist. Off to the south, its white stone peak capped by a single cloud, Mont Ventoux rises high above the surrounding landscape.

When I first contemplated doing this, I thought I would feel like Rocky Balboa after he ran up the stairs in Philadelphia and turned to raise his arms in defiant triumph. Instead I am feeling contented and solitary on a mountaintop.

Coasting down Garde Grosse is almost like soaring, and that matches the mood I am in. There is a weightless feeling about a downhill descent, so much so that I enter the first corner too fast and have to brake hard. It is a steep curve and the wheels skid and almost lock up. The morning air now feels cool—I'm no longer labouring uphill and building body heat. I stop to zip up my top and start again, this time more slowly in order to enjoy the ride. No longer toiling with my head to the handlebars, it is easier to take in the terrain.

The upper part of the mountain is forested, a preserve for deer and wild boar, and in the fall the villagers come here for the mushrooms. Partway down, on the gentler slopes, the farms appear—it's too high to grow the crops that thrive in the valley below. Sheep and goats once populated these cleared green fields, but today they are largely devoid of farm animals; perhaps that was too much work, and with government handouts there is less need for farmers to produce their own food. All the same, I pass a few goats meandering in fenced enclosures. It's possible these are the ones that provide the milk for the cheese my wife buys from her cheese seller at the Thursday market. I pass old tilleul trees harvested for their flowers to make herbal teas. Lower down, small orchards of fruit trees replace the goats, but it is still too high for growing grapes.

The descent goes fast, and surprisingly quickly I am on the winding lanes with houses on either side, and then on the highway alongside the Aygues River. This time I cross on the ancient Roman Pont that spans the river in a single stone arch of forty metres. I stop and knock at the door of the *pâtisserie* before the owner opens for the day, and *madame* comes away from her oven to unlock the door and sell me hot croissants.

When I arrive at the *tabac* for the *Trib*, the owner is cutting the plastic bands holding the bundles of newspapers.

It is still early morning as I cycle on through the village and home, and I am elated.

The following morning I had stepped out of the shower and was drying myself with the bathroom door open when Hélène walked by and stopped to stare.

"What the *hell!* What happened to *you?*"

I looked down at a black-violet bruise that was spreading between my legs and at the scrape from hip to ankle on my right leg. To my surprise I responded by smiling foolishly. She saw the look on my face and shook her head before walking away.

*   *   *

I should have realized that François was an unusual person, but I hadn't properly taken in the signs. I had seen his determination to finish a task when he had cut out a tree stump with a small hatchet. That was at odds with his seemingly fine physique and quiet temperament. He was always a gentle, soft-spoken person who knew every plant, shrub and tree in our garden. He could talk about each one, not as species or by Latin names, but by its habits, its particular need for sun, water and the season it showed best in. If I asked him about some plant, he would invariably tell me where in the garden it would do best and vigorously disagree if I suggested the wrong place.

Once when I asked François a question he didn't have a ready answer for, the next time we met he reminded me of my question and had the answer. He never spoke badly of anyone. Of a particularly lazy man his only comment was, "*Il est spéciale*"—he is different. He didn't seem to have an aggressive or competitive side to him, just a straightforward sense of honesty. He showed a harmony and comfort with nature that bordered on respect. One day a particularly large and dangerous jet-black wasp—almost three centimetres long—landed near me and began making the same angry noise as an Apache attack helicopter. "*Une mauvaise guêpe—très dangereuse*," he said, and, instead of harming it, he simply waved it off and watched it fly away.

Even though François rarely talked about his passion, I knew that, like so many Frenchmen, he liked cycling.

Hélène said to me, "You should tell François about your climb of Garde Grosse. It would give you something in common to talk about."

I tucked the idea away in the back of my mind, rather liking it. The opportunity arose when he and his wife, Manon, invited us over to their home once again, this time for Sunday lunch.

After the second course, we were sipping our wine when Manon came back from the kitchen carrying more plates. She was gay and talkative.

"I picked up François after the race last weekend. It was next to impossible to find him amid the hundreds of cyclists and the crowd of spectators at the finish line. But he had seen our van and walked over before I saw him. He loaded his *vélo* in the back, closed the door and was getting in the passenger seat next to me when I noticed that people were opening the rear doors of the van and putting bouquets of flowers on the back seat. 'What's this?' I asked.

"François just smiled at me and said, 'They're for the winner.'"

"I sat there in the driver's seat for a second, wondering what he was talking about. 'So why are they putting the flowers in our van?'"

"He thought that was funny. . . . 'I won the race.' He said it so casually that I still didn't quite get it."

"'You won the race?'" Manon repeated, stopping for a moment to laugh at herself.

François just smiled at her.

He even looked a bit awkward at the attention he was getting, so I asked him, "What was the race?"

Manon answered for him. "Oh, it was the ascent of Mont Ventoux."

I was speechless. . . . It took Hélène to leap in with a toast. *"Au champion de Mont Ventoux, le Géant de Provence!"*

We raised our glasses to François, who was looking down with his usual humility. However, Manon wasn't quite ready to let go of the subject.

"Venez"—come, she said, and she got up and led us into the hallway. *"Ce sont ses trophées de vélos,"* she said, pointing at a large cabinet while François stood in silence behind us.

The cabinet was filled with trophies; they overflowed onto the top until they almost touched the ceiling.

On the drive home after lunch Hélène said, "I thought you were going to tell François about your climb of Garde Grosse?"

"Some other time, maybe." *Normalement*, I thought, meaning it was unlikely I'd ever raise the subject again. I'd worked in the garden with the king of mountain racing and hadn't even known it.

"That was quite a story Manon told us," she said.

"Yes, it was," I replied.

Chapter 17
a celebrity bird ~ or how to cook a French icon

It is difficult to think of anything more symbolically French than the Bresse chicken. After all, it is a bird naturally born with the colours of the French flag: its coxcomb is red, its feathers pure white and its legs blue—French from top to bottom. Whether or not that has anything to do with it becoming one of France's greatest gastronomic triumphs is unclear, but all the same, its stellar standing is unimpeachable. Poulet de Bresse struts its stuff. Without a doubt, it is both a culinary and a cultural success story.

This bird reached cult status (up in the same stratosphere as Johnny Hallyday, the French equivalent of Elvis Presley) when the great French chef Paul Bocuse of Lyon made Poulet de Bresse his signature dish. And so the French adopted it as a symbol of French culinary excellence. Like any other national treasure, every aspect of the bird's life is controlled by the state, and in France that means all the way from its conception as an egg to its fate at the dinner table. There is even a designated 'Selection Centre' to ensure healthy stock and genetic purity, thereby assuring that nothing can spoil a good thing. In all likelihood, these birds get better national health care than the citizens of France. Once hatched under the most controlled of circumstances, each is entitled to a diet of maize, wheat and milk and its fill of grass, worms, insects and whatever else can be foraged from its own private ten square metres of designated turf. Can a Parisian claim the same pampered quality of life?

Not to miss out on a promotional opportunity, the farmers who raise these birds were quick to call them 'the Queen of Poultry, the Poultry of Kings'. In 1957, the President of France, René Coty, enacted a law recognizing 'Volaille de Bresse' as a gastronomic wonder that needed protection under the renowned French *appellation d'origine contrôlée* system (AOC). From that day forward a Bresse chicken was 'guaranteed' by the state. Quite an elevated status for a mere chicken, some might say. However, the AOC does ensure that this poultry has only been raised on the geologically correct *terroir* in accordance with extraordinarily strict procedures and laws. When it comes to their foods, the French become very paternal.

Bresse lies near Lyon, in the northern Rhône Valley that is considered to be the culinary centre of France. There are roughly 205 approved breeders producing some 1.2 million Bresse chickens each year. Statistics show that thirty to forty per cent are sent to Paris, fifty-five to sixty-five per cent to other parts of France and only five per cent are ever shipped abroad. Not that long ago, as proof of its origin, the poultry had to be wrapped in linen or cotton with some white feathers protruding, but this swaddling practice has changed for the less labour-demanding use of white plastic.

It should be understood that not all poultry from Bresse is 'Volailles de Bresse', as other birds are also raised there. To be sure there is no confusion, measures have been taken to clearly identify the real thing by attaching a metal ring on its left leg (unfortunately not gold) bearing the name and address of the rearer. As further irrefutable proof of its authenticity a red-white-and-blue seal is attached to the neck, giving the name of the agent that prepared the bird. However, despite all these precautions, that still does not mean the diner can be entirely sure of the bird's provenance, for one hapless French chef made the ghastly mistake of passing off ordinary chicken as 'Volaille de Bresse' in his restaurant. When caught at his crime, he was indignantly drummed out of business and retired in shame.

So, one has to ask, what is it about a Bresse chicken that sets it apart from all others? A little research informed me that it has a fine white flesh marbled with fat from its special diet, and a rich, gamey flavour that comes from its foraging on anything small that flies or crawls on its patch of soil. When seared and roasted so that the bird cooks 'within itself' (retaining its juices inside the golden skin), it produces a moist and uniquely delicious dining experience.

This description alone convinced us to try it; however, we weren't planning to travel north to the Bresse region or dine at Paul Bocuse's three-star Michelin restaurant, and none of the local restaurants offered the dish. The only solution was to buy a Poulet de Bresse and cook it ourselves.

"I can't live in France without trying one of the most famous dishes this country has every created," Hélène pronounced. "Besides, we owe dinner invitations to Jean and Suzette, François and Manon, Marcel and his wife. Think about the dinners they put on for us. This dish may do it."

She telephoned invitations for the following Friday and set to planning the dinner. A recipe was found on the Internet. The photo posted beside the recipe was of a man dressed entirely in white with a ribbon around his neck bearing the French tricolour that I now associated with the French flag as well as a chicken.

We drove into the village and, while Hélène was inside talking to the butcher, I went off to buy the best white wines I could find at a specialty wine store near the arcade. I came back with bottles of Mâcon white, champagne and some staggeringly expensive Corton-Charlemagne that the proprietor assured me was an excellent vintage from one of the best winemakers in Burgundy. When I returned, Hélène was standing in front of the shop with bags of food, grinning happily.

"Was I ever lucky! The butcher said Bresse chicken is hard to get and had to be ordered in advance. Then he smiled at me and went to the back of his shop and returned with one. He said it was for another customer, but I could have it. He'd just tell her it would take a few more days for hers to come in."

We drove home and struggled into the house, weighed down with bags of food and bottles of wine.

On Friday morning Hélène entered the kitchen with more than her usual culinary anxiety. The dinner had to come off perfectly, she said, or she would not be considered a *femme sérieuse*—someone able to cook to the French standard our guests viewed as normal. The kitchen bustled with activity. Slowly, as the day's creative efforts progressed, it became the centre of a rich assortment of aromas. The oven was hot, pots gave off steam on the stove, used pans were cleaned and put away again. The champagne, the Mâcon and the Corton-Charlemagne were cooling in the fridge. I set the table, and with the kitchen now under control, we both retired to shower. A sense of tense well-being was in the air.

The French dine late by North American standards, so we had suggested our guests arrive at 7:30. Nevertheless, our timing was running a bit off, and we were still dressing when the doorbell rang. I saw my wife straighten up, her eyes focused in the distance—no doubt thinking about what still had to be done or what she might have forgotten. She had the tight look of a person about to make her first professional appearance before her peers. Only then did I realize how important this dinner was to her. Glancing out the back window I could see François and Manon at our gate, so I quickly buttoned my shirt as I descended the stairs to greet them.

As it was an unusually warm day for so late in the fall, I had set up chairs on the patio for *apéros*. By chance, Jean and Suzette as well as Marcel and his wife arrived at the same time, and introductions were made as I popped the champagne corks. Hélène passed trays of smoked salmon with capers on freshly toasted rounds of baguette and Nyons tapenade on crackers. After tasting the champagne, our guests immediately relaxed and the conversation began to flow. In the fading evening light, we moved indoors for dinner.

The first course was an eggplant, red pepper and onion mousse topped with *crème fraîche* and served on a bed of baby lettuce leaves. I poured the Mâcon white wine. When that course was finished, I removed the plates and poured the Corton-Charlemagne while Hélène brought the main course to the table. By the time she sat down, the conversation had slowed as everyone had begun studying the plates before them. We picked up our cutlery and commenced.

The bird proved plump and moist; a cream sauce (which Hélène had altered by adding Marcel's truffles) covered the crisp golden skin and pooled in a corner of the plate. Thin strips of green onion separated the chicken from the puréed potato, and barely-cooked baby carrots were splayed nearby.

Suzette ate a morsel of the chicken, stopped and looked at my wife. "*C'est un* Poulet de Bresse!" she exclaimed. "*La sauce aux truffes est extraordinaire!*"

Coming from an experienced cook like Suzette, that was a telling compliment, and Hélène looked up, radiant, her tension suddenly melting away. "*Merci,*" was all she was able to say before Jean raised his glass.

"*Au chef!*" he pronounced.

We took our first sip of the Corton-Charlemagne, and once more the conversation paused for a moment before quickly becoming even more animated and festive.

Suzette had prepared a pear tart with a glazed finish for dessert, and Manon had brought a selection of cheeses from nearby farms. I opened a bottle of very cold Muscat de Beaumes de Venice from Domaine Durban. Coffee followed, served strong and with a selection of *petits fours*. Everyone was having so much fun that I brought out more glasses to pour a *digestif* of Génépi Le Chamois, the highly intoxicating green-tinted herbal liquor from the Savoy region. Conversation continued as if it would never end. It remained boisterous all the way out the driveway in the sweet night air sometime well after midnight. After cheeks were kissed three times and hugs happily exchanged all around, our guests left for their respective homes.

As we re-entered the house, Hélène spun around and gave me a hug.

"Congratulations," I said.

"Thank you!" And with that she almost danced up the staircase and went to bed.

I cleared the dining room table and gathered the linen for washing the next day. After loading the dishwasher I set the remaining pots and pans in the sink to soak. The rest could wait till morning. I stepped out onto the balcony and gazed down at the lights that dotted the sleeping village below and up at the stars above, and then I followed to bed.

Chapter 18
vineyard toil ~ finding Provence

To have advanced true friends . . .

THE MORNING WAS OVERCAST and ominous, with grey clouds scurrying across the sky, when Pierre Luc arrived at our front door. His face had a haunted look. His normally abundant self-assurance was missing, and his eyes glistened and darted wildly. He hesitated before speaking.

"*Êtes-vous libre? J'ai besoin d'assistance.*"

His words had none of their normal carefree manner. He was asking for my help.

"*Pourquoi?*" I asked, expecting to hear about an illness or disaster at his house.

"*Il va pleuvoir!*" he said, blurting out the words.

I looked at the sky. Yes, it looked like rain was coming. But what was so serious about a little rain? Then the penny dropped. His grapes hadn't been harvested. He'd spent all summer half-heartedly tending his vineyards as if the success of his new venture had somehow been assured. Now it was about to rain.

Pierre Luc stood looking at me, waiting for me to say something.

"You want me to help with the grape-harvest?" I asked incredulously, remembering the hard work of helping Monsieur Ladoux with his vineyard last fall—an experience I did not care to repeat. It had been backbreaking, tedious labour with none of the romantic appeal that I had expected.

The tight expression on Pierre Luc's face hardly eased. "*Oui, si possible.*"

He had never asked anything of me. It was just not done in Provence. A man had to be independent here; self-sufficiency was a matter of pride. Individuals had to be able to look after their own affairs. In the past, Pierre Luc had gotten around this by offering to show me how to tend a vineyard. But now he was straight-out asking for my help.

"*Quand?*"—when?

"*Maintenant!*"—now!

For a brief moment I thought about making up some excuse, or simply saying no, but Pierre Luc was standing there looking at me.

"*D'accord. J'arrive dans quinze minutes*"—I'll be there in fifteen minutes, I said.

I went upstairs to tell Hélène and to change my clothing.

"This is a race against the weather," I explained.

"You did this last year. Don't you remember how hard it was?"

"So what am I to do?"

She didn't speak for a few moments. "Is it that serious for him?"

"I expect it's about his livelihood. If he can't save the vintage, he'll lose his farm. He's in debt. The bank won't extend another year of credit."

I could see that she was thinking. She looked away for a moment, and in that instant she made up her mind. "Then I'm coming with you."

When we reached their house, Pierre Luc and Jules were already working at the bottom of the vineyard. Hélène went to the door of the house, knocked and went in. I walked over to join the two men. Jules was speaking angrily to Pierre Luc in what must have been Provençal, for I didn't understand a word. When Jules saw me approaching, he stopped talking and I felt that same appraising glance he had given me in the spring.

"Jules has finished his harvest," Pierre Luc said, "so he'll work here with us. I've put a hopper halfway up the vineyard, so we don't have to walk as far to empty our *panniers*. It's got a canvas cover against the rain."

He handed me a pair of *sécateurs* and a basket. "*Maintenant, allons-y, allons-y!*"—let's get at it, *now*!

Pierre Luc's panic was obvious.

I looked at the task ahead of us—two small vineyards of about three acres, or just over a hectare in all, had to be harvested before the impending rain. *Where were his bar friends?* I wondered. However, that was beside the point. All the three of us could do was start and see how much we could harvest before the rain came. I took one look at the rows of vines mounting up the hillside, then lifted the cone-shaped basket onto my back, fitted the straps over my shoulders and joined the two of them at work. *After all*, I thought, *I have done it before.*

At mid-afternoon Hélène came out with Orangina to drink and sandwiches. "Pierre Luc's wife is almost hysterical. She says he should have begun the harvest days ago but didn't get around to it."

We gathered together in one of the rows of the vineyard and stood eating rapidly. Jules waved away a glass of Orangina and sipped from his small wine keg instead. We returned to work, moving up the slope where the vineyard became progressively steeper. It was becoming harder to see because of the darkening sky.

The rain began as a gentle falling mist that slowly intensified. It even felt warm, possibly from the energy I was expending. When it became a steady drizzle, Hélène returned with rain gear for all of us. She also brought flashlights. "It will be dark soon."

I had worn my black *vigneron*'s hat from last fall, but its broad brim absorbed the rain and folded down and became useless. Hélène saw the problem and brought out a cotton sun hat with a two-inch brim that kept the rain off my face. All the same, the situation seemed ridiculously difficult. Trying to hold the flashlight in one hand while cutting a grape bunch with the other and then catching the falling bunch was next to impossible.

Furthermore, with the light rain the soil was turning to the consistency of grease. At one point my foot slid out from under me and I went down, spilling the contents of my basket. I grappled for the flashlight and stood up, slipping on both feet before finding my balance and then picking up the muddy bunches of grapes that had fallen from my basket.

Then I saw Pierre Luc walk out of the vineyard. *It's over*, I thought, and began to follow him. But he didn't go the house. He went into the shed, and I heard an engine cough to life then saw a tractor come out with its lights on. As he drove up the slope, the tractor lost traction and slewed sideways for a foot in the mud. He changed gears and found traction again, inching the machine between two rows of vines, then stopped where we had been working. Fortunately the rows ran across rather than vertically on the slope and the tractor found sufficient grip.

"*Venez!*"—come here, he hollered. We went back to work in the steady drizzle in the glare of the lights from the tractor with the mechanical throb of its engine in our ears.

We just kept working, even though the rain must have already ruined the grapes. All the same, Pierre Luc and Jules were not letting up, and I couldn't walk away and leave them. I wanted to quit, but if they would not, then neither would I. I wondered where Pierre Luc found this unexpected drive. As for me, whenever I become involved in a repetitious physical job my brain shuts down and the task becomes one long, mindless chore, as if nothing else exists or matters.

Through the long night that followed, Hélène and Fanny took turns bringing us food and hot drinks. We used these brief periods to rest and recover enough energy to keep on working. We just kept at it: pushing back the leaves to reveal the grape-clusters, cutting them out, moving the tractor along the rows to illuminate the vines ahead of us, emptying our baskets into the hoppers, as we worked our way along each row and up the vineyard until the sky began to lighten.

When Pierre Luc's vineyard was harvested, he took the tractor around the curve of the hill to the adjacent vineyard he'd leased, and we worked our way back down the hill this time. There was no real dawn, just a gradual lightening in the grey sky. By late morning, the last row had been harvested. All of us were sombre, exhausted and uncommunicative. The best we could manage were stiff smiles to acknowledge the grapes were in. Any more animated expression would have been far too difficult. Hélène and I walked home in the rain.

•   •   •

After the marathon grape-picking, I took it easy for three or four days, letting my body recover, going to bed early and rising late. I was too stiff and tired to ride my bike and even too mentally fatigued to work on my book.

One day when Hélène had gone shopping, I began reading a light novel set in Provence about the heist of a Cézanne painting. Then, tiring of the novel, I had gone down to the garage looking for a project to occupy myself. Before I could find one I heard a voice at the door.

"May I come in?"

It was Pierre Luc with his dog, Fidel. My mind went back to his last unexpected visit, and I wondered what could have gone wrong now—bad news about the harvest?

"Yes, of course," I answered, walking over to open the door wider.

Pierre Luc looked exhausted, yet surprisingly calm. "We crushed the grapes at Jules' place. He has a wine press. In a few days we will separate the skins, seeds and stems from the juice. I've also been helping Jules. I owe it to him."

"It's been a disaster for you." I said it a bit too hastily and glanced at him for his reaction.

"No—no, it's not! It's okay. Really."

His manner wasn't as downbeat as I expected—he was not showing the abject despair he had shown when he'd asked for my help.

"But we picked in the pouring rain," I said. "The grapes—"

"After you left, we did a test of the sugar level in the grapes and we got them just in time."

He must have seen scepticism on my face for he added, "Yes, yes, but it takes time for the water to reach the grapes. We're going to be fine. There's enough concentration in the grapes to make a good wine. We *just* caught it in time," he repeated.

He was exhausted and dirty from days of harvesting and crushing grapes, but his face showed a calm I hadn't seen in him before.

"*Merci,*" he said, reaching out to shake my hand, and then, so spontaneously that I was taken aback, he hugged me, slapped me hard on the back and said, "*Mon pote.*"

I went stiff with surprise and without thinking hugged him right back. "*De rien*"—it's nothing, was all I managed to say.

He had called me his best friend—*mon pote*. In those few words I felt an appreciation, a comradeship, in the work we shared together. This was not at all like the previous fall when I had helped M. Ladoux—that had been prompted by my own self-interest to learn about the vineyards of Provence.

"I want you to come with me," Pierre Luc said.

"Where to?"

"My uncle Jules' place, where the wine is being made."

"Okay," I nodded.

Pierre Luc's green 2CV was at the gate. We got in, Fidel in the back where he sat up on one seat and looked around. I sat next to Pierre Luc on a canvas seat made like a garden chair that swung as we drove through Nyons and into the hills to the east.

"My father," Pierre Luc said, "planted the vineyards, and, as a boy, I thought it was wonderful. But nobody wanted a new grape variety here. So he couldn't sell the wine he made. The next year he was forced to sell the grapes to the cooperative for next to nothing. He finally quit as there was no money in it. He lost his enthusiasm for life."

We drove on some distance in silence, and then Pierre Luc began talking again.

"D'you know, I almost gave up too, when the rain came. I remembered my father's failure and saw no point in trying. For me, trying just meant failure. It frightened me at first, and then I got angry."

He stopped there and didn't say any more.

After about half an hour we turned off the road and went up a side road to an old stone farm building, where he stopped. Jules must have heard the car arrive, for just at that moment he stepped out of the building and came over to greet us. Now I was in for my second surprise, for he shook my hand and looked me squarely in the eye. His hand was as leathery as his sun-worn complexion. Having done that, he abruptly turned and strode away toward his house, leaving Pierre Luc and me standing there.

Inside the stone building I saw six or seven large fermentation tanks.

"I will sleep with my wine," Pierre Luc was already saying. "I have a bed near the vats, and I will open the doors at night

189

to let in the cool air and close them during the day to keep the heat out. White wines must ferment in cool conditions over long weeks to protect their aroma and delicate tastes from too much heat. I will listen to them ferment and watch that all is well. Fanny helps with the work, gives me advice about the fermentation."

He showed me which vats contained his fermenting wine, the equipment and went on to describe what had to be done.

"My wife knows a lot about all the technical stuff," he said. "Her training at L'Université du Vin has been very good. She says the skins must be left in the fermentation tank just long enough to pick up colour and enhance the flavours of the wine. After the grapes are crushed, sulphur dioxide is added to prevent oxidation. It has to be watched every day. It can take two months to convert the sugar to alcohol. I'm learning.

"All week she drops Violette off at school and then she comes up and the two of us work together. On weekends Violette comes with us and helps out, or plays with the children in Rochebrune." He paused, as if deciding whether to go on.

"I don't really know why people make such a fuss about wine. It's just fermented grape juice. If I can have my farm and my family, and earn a living making very good wine, that is enough."

We drove back to Nyons and he stopped the 2CV at my gate.

"Do you have time for a glass of wine?" I asked.

"Is it a good wine?"

"Let's have a look. You know I have some from the vineyard next door. Do you know *Monsieur* Ladoux?"

"*Mais oui!* He makes good wine."

"Let's try one from last year's vintage. I can tell you all about it."

I motioned to Pierre Luc to pull out two chairs from the garden furniture I had moved into the garage for the winter. I brought out several bottles, uncorking one.

Fidel was asleep under the table when Hélène drove up and walked into the garage. Pierre Luc immediately stood up to greet her, blowing the usual kisses past her cheeks. I saw her glance at the open bottle on the table and the empty one on the floor.

After Pierre Luc left and I went upstairs, Hélène said, "You two were having a good time down there. What's up?"

I told her about the afternoon.

"Yes, Pierre Luc does look different—somehow more sure of himself."

"He has accomplished something," I said.

Chapter 19
autumn leaves

FALL HAD SNUCK UP on us, as seasons can. One day it was warm and sunny, the following morning, without forewarning, there was a cold bite to the air. It happened a month after the grape harvest and reminded me that we were well into October. The days were much shorter and the sun lower in the sky. The fading colours, greyer tones, longer shadows and the calm that sometimes accompanies cooler weather signalled that the year was coming to an end.

When we arrived for the Thursday *marché*, the merchants were standing with their hands stuffed in their coat pockets waiting for the shoppers. The fall vegetables that were used for making hearty soups and stews had arrived, as well as a full range of wild mushrooms scavenged from the forest floors (muddy and stacked in piles by species), ready to be picked over by the local shoppers. The *marché* had shrunk back to its normal size as the last of the city vacationers and tourists had returned home. All the same, a few stalls were actually busier than usual. A group of men were gathered around a man selling camouflage clothing that blended with the patchy trunks of the nearby plane trees. We had already heard the distant pop of guns in the forested parts of the hill behind our villa.

"A very good fall for truffles," François said when he came to do his fall clean-up of our garden. He was referring to the September rains that put water in the soil for the truffles to grow. I finally told him about my ride up Mont Garde Grosse, and his only response was his usual friendly smile. But before he left that day, I saw him looking over my all-purpose bike in the garage.

I had not seen much of Pierre Luc and his wife since his visit after the harvest, though occasionally the green 2CV dashed by our house on its way somewhere. When he did drop in one day, he said winemaking required a lot of hard work. He didn't stay long. I could tell he had other things on his mind.

•   •   •

I had spent the spring and summer reading about Provence and visiting its famous sites—from the Romans to the Middle Ages and getting to know its artists and writers—and I was busy putting my books on Provence back into the armoire when Hélène came in.

"You've stopped reading about Provence," she said.

"I guess we don't live in history."

"Hmm," she said.

"I've been trying to see Provence through its history and the eyes of its artists. Sure, we toured the sites, but living in Provence is not about that. It's about living in a community with people. We are fortunate, because that community is right here, in—of all places—Provence."

She didn't say anything, so I continued.

"You know, helping M. Ladoux in his vineyard last year was a pretty touristy thing to do. It wasn't until I had to help out Pierre Luc that I learned what it takes to live somewhere."

She was still silent, but I could tell she was taking in what I said.

"Pierre Luc changed my outlook. After helping him with his harvest, I felt I was not just an outside observer. I was a part of the way of life here."

"So, do you want to own a vineyard?"

"No way, but I want to write about it."

"Lunch will be ready in a few minutes," she said as she left the room smiling.

We felt and heard the shriek of the mistral that night, the wind that sweeps the Rhône Valley with a witch's broom, bending trees sideways and laying waste to anything not anchored to the ground. By morning it had blown away the clouds and the hard blue sky of fall was back.

*   *   *

In the cooler days of autumn the air was crisp and pleasant to breathe. I rode my bike through the village, over the bridge and through the tunnel and continued east alongside the Aygues River, following it into the Pre-Alps, and toward the remote village of Tarendol. The road ran through the villages of Aubres and then Les Piles, and then past Curnier and Arpavon, where François and Manon lived, and finally past Ste-Jalle. From there the land opens out onto a broad valley. A grand vista of countryside appears—a patchwork of fields interspersed with lavender, fruit and olive orchards, and vineyards that reach high up the sides of the hills. I had driven through the area once before, on the skiing trip with Jean in the spring.

When I had first taken up riding, I had realized that I could speed along taking in things in a way that driving in a car could not match, for I felt immersed in a moving three-dimensional paranoma where the countryside was always changing and the scents and sounds actually related to the sights.

The valley tilts upward to the east making the terrain visible ahead, as if a map was unfolding before me as I rode. Tarendol sits high up a hill at the farthest end of this valley. While the gentle upward grade of the road was not demanding, it slowed my progress, adding more time to the ride than I had anticipated. The leaves high on the hillsides were turning to hues of rust and yellow. When I finally made it to the easterly end of the valley and saw the steep road leading up to Tarendol, I braced for the toughest part of the ride.

The village proved to be smaller than I had expected, more a hilltop hamlet of only a dozen or so houses. A tiny church, scaled down to the needs of the village, stood next to a walled graveyard that offered a stunning view to the valley far below. A string of rusty poles with antique lanterns marked the entry to the single street. It wasn't really a street, in fact, for the hamlet sat on an elbow in the road that passed through and ran on into the remote hills behind. Coming out the other side of the elbow, I realized I had ridden through Tarendol. Aside from a few vehicles, I felt I had stepped backward in time a century or two. The houses appeared awkward and out of place in the barren landscape. There were no vineyards in sight, probably due to the much higher altitude.

I stopped and looked around, half-hoping in this remote place to see something showing speaking to the roots of the famous writer René Barjavel, but this now seemed very unlikely. He had written his autobiography about growing up in Nyons a century ago. His grandfather had lived in Tarendol, and when his son was fifteen years of age the grandfather had walked the boy roughly fifty kilometres to Nyons so he could apprentice as a *boulanger*. The boy was hired, and so the man left his son and walked back home the same day.

I turned around and coasted downhill, past the houses once more, and slowly began to enjoy the tranquil autumn scene that bore no sign of movement anywhere. Then, about halfway down the hill I saw another rider, really just a dot in the distance, biking up the hill and setting a surprisingly fast pace. When we were closer, he saw me and stopped, so I glided down until I was next to him and stopped too. We talked for some time. He said he used these hills regularly for training.

After we parted, I found the ride back to Nyons remarkably easy as it was almost entirely downhill. When I reached home Hélène was putting jars on the top shelf of the kitchen cupboard.

"What's that?" I asked.

"I spent the day with Suzette making jelly and *pâte de coing*."

She saw my quizzical look.

"*Coing* is a quince. We've driven by orchards of it on the way to Vaison-la-Romaine. It's the shape of a pear, but so hard and bitter that it's almost impossible to eat raw. So invariably it's made into a preserve. The result can be a marvellously sharp jelly or a rich paste as thick as peanut butter, or it's even added to apple sauce. Suzette uses lots of lemon and lemon zest to sharpen the flavour. I told you about it in the summer."

I listened, and then told her about the ride to Tarendol and meeting the other rider.

"François says he'll take me to a *marchand de cycles* tomorrow that sells les *vélos* in Aubres and help me buy a road bike. He says it has to be fitted to the body type of the rider for leg and arm length, almost tailored to measure."

"Wonderful," she said. "And before you go, we can taste this quince jelly when you get the croissants in the morning."

•   •   •

A trace of snow had appeared on Garde Grosse overnight. It did not last the day, but it spoke about the season. We had observed the cool green in the vineyards being replaced by the brighter colours of fall. Then, after that last quick burst of colour, the falling leaves were like a gasp, forewarning us of the icy winds soon to follow. The rigid rows of gnarly vine trunks would stand mute again against the ashen tones of winter.

In the village, leaves blanketed the square, rustling under our feet, lifting and stirring with an invisible wind as if brought momentarily back to life for one last breath, reminding us with each step that the warm days of summer had gone for the year. There was a different quality to the air, a musty dryness, empty of the richer scents of summer; it brought to mind things completed and at an end. The calendar year ends in midwinter, long before spring brings a burst of growth, and its own new year.

Is it so small a thing
To have enjoyed the sun,
To have lived light in the spring,
To have loved, to have thought, to have done;
To have advanced true friends . . .

—Matthew Arnold, *Empedocles on Etna*

APPENDICES

Reading the French Menu

carte ~ menu

carte des vins ~ wine list

entrée ~ main course that may be ordered alone

menu complet ~ set of courses that may include an appetizer, main course, dessert, a quart or quarter litre of wine; each restaurant or bistro will be a bit different

menu du jour ~ special set of courses the establishment offers that day; often the best value and the best quality as it is fresh

plateau de fromage ~ selection of cheeses on a platter that will be brought to the table after the main course and before the dessert

prix fixe menu ~ generally the special menu of the day is posted at the door; for lunch it normally includes an appetizer and main course, or the main course and dessert (and often a quart of wine); for dinner it is normally three or four courses

soupe du jour ~ soup of the day

How would you like your steak?

cuit ~ cooked:
- *bleu* ~ very rare
- *saignant* ~ rare
- *à point* ~ medium
- *bien cuit(e)* ~ well done

Appetizers

amuse-bouche ~ appetizer at beginning of meal to whet the appetite (palate amusement)

canapé ~ small piece of bread with a savoury topping served at receptions

hors-d'oeuvre ~ small savoury item served before a meal to stimulate the appetite (literally means 'outside work')

Meats & Meat Dishes

agneau ~ lamb

boeuf ~ beef

gigot ~ leg of lamb or mutton

brebis ~ lamb, ewe

charcuterie ~ assortment of cold meats

chèvre ~ goat

chevreuil ~ venison

côtes ~ chops, ribs (cutlets)

entrecôte ~ rib steak; a superior steak than that which is used for *steak frites*

faux-fillet ~ a not-so-tender cut of sirloin beef

jambon ~ ham

lapin ~ rabbit

lardons ~ cubed bacon

lièvre ~ hare

noisette ~ a hazelnut, but also a small round steak, frequently of lamb or mutton

porc ~ pork

roulade ~ a preparation, a thin slice of meat that is stuffed and rolled

sanglier ~ wild boar

saucisse, saucisson ~ sausage

steak frites ~ steak and french fries; also see *entrecôte*

veau ~ veal

viande ~ meat

Seafood

anchois ~ anchovy

anguille ~ eel

baudroie ~ monkfish (also *lotte*)

cabillaud ~ cod

calmar ~ squid

crevette ~ shrimp or prawn

daurade ~ Mediterranean sea bream

huître ~ oyster

langoustine ~ small lobster-like crustacean

loup de mer ~ sea bass (*bar*)

maquereau ~ mackerel

morue ~ salt cod (*cabillaud*)

moule ~ mussel

poisson ~ fish

rouget ~ red mullet

saumon ~ salmon

thon ~ tuna

Fowl

canard – duck
caille – quail
dinde – turkey
oie – goose
pintade – guinea fowl
poule – hen
poulet – chicken (*coq* – rooster)
poulet fermier – free-range chicken
poulet de Bresse – famous French chicken fed mostly on selected foods such as corn and buckwheat
volaille – poultry

Baked Goods

baguette – white bread, long and thin, crisp crust
baton – a small baguette
boulangerie – bakery; a *boulanger* is the baker
croissant – fine, crescent shaped flaky pastry
croûton – crisp bit of bread
ficelle – very thin version of a baguette
fougasse – flat loaf, sometimes with filling added
gressin – breadstick
pain – bread
  - *pain de campagne* – country, rustic
  - *pain complet* – wholewheat
  - *pain de levain* – sourdough
  - *pain au chocolat* – croissant with chocolate filling
pâtisserie – pastry or cake shop, as opposed to a *boulangerie*, which specializes in breads and croissants (the two often overlap each other); a *pâtissier* is the pastry chef

Nuts
amande ~ almond
cacahuète ~ peanut (*arachide*)
cajou ~ cashew
châtaignier ~ chestnut (*marron*)
noisette ~ hazelnut
noix ~ walnut
noix de pecan ~ pecan
pignon ~ pine nut

Dairy
beurre ~ butter
chèvre ~ goat, goat's cheese
crème ~ cream
crème fraîche ~ thick and sharp fresh cream slightly soured
vache ~ cow
fromage ~ cheese
lait ~ milk
yaourt ~ yogurt

Vegetables
ail ~ garlic
artichaut ~ artichoke
asperge ~ asparagus
carotte ~ carrot
ciboule ~ scallion (green onion)
céleri ~ celery
céleri-rave ~ celeriac (celery root)
ciboulette ~ chive
courgette ~ zucchini
crudités ~ raw vegetables

échalote ~ shallot
épinards ~ spinach
fève ~ fava bean
frites ~ chips (GB); french fries (USA)
haricots vert ~ green beans
panais ~ parsnip
poivron ~ sweet pepper
pomme de terre ~ potato
poireau ~ leek
tomate ~ tomato

Fruit

abricot ~ apricot
cassis ~ blackcurrant
cerise ~ cherry
citron ~ lemon
coing ~ quince
figue ~ fig
fraise ~ strawberry
framboise ~ raspberry
mûre ~ blackberry
myrtille ~ blueberry
pamplemousse ~ grapefruit
pêche ~ peach
poire ~ pear
pomme ~ apple
radis ~ radish
tanche ~ olive specific to the area around Nyons; meaty and
nutty characteristics

Mayonnaise, Pastes, Sauces & Purées

aïoli ~ sauce made of eggs, garlic and olive oil whipped to the texture of mayonnaise

anchoïade ~ savoury paste made by mashing anchovies, olive oil and garlic

brandade ~ purée of garlic, salt cod and cream, and often olive oil

coulis ~ purée, usually of fruit

fricassée ~ meat (often fowl) that has been cut into pieces, then fried or stewed and served in a white sauce

pistou ~ sauce made with basil, garlic and olive oil; in Italy pine nuts are added and it is called pesto

purée ~ fruit or vegetable crushed and blended into a cream-like texture

rouille ~ garlic mayonnaise with red chillies and sometimes saffron; served with seafood dishes such as *bouillabaisse*

tapenade ~ paste made from olives, olive oil and capers; used as a spread on toast like a *canapé*; anchovies may be added

Herbs, Spices & Seasonings

aneth ~ dill

aromate ~ herbs referred to as 'aromatic' due to their distinct scents

anis ~ anise seed, used for pastis

basilic ~ basil

câpre ~ caper

coriandre ~ coriander (cilantro)

estragon ~ tarragon

fenouil ~ fennel

feuille de laurier ~ bay leaf

girofle ~ clove

herbe ~ herb; leaves, seeds or flowers of plants which impart flavouring, perfume and sometimes medicinal properties

herbes de Provence ~ mixture of thyme, rosemary, bay basil, savory and sometimes lavender; available throughout Provence

lavande ~ lavender; not truly an herb, but an aromatic

marjolaine ~ marjoram

menthe ~ mint

moutarde ~ mustard

persil ~ parsley

poivre ~ pepper

romarin ~ rosemary

sarriette ~ summer savoury

sauge ~ sage

sel ~ salt

thym ~ thyme

Temperature

fraîche(f) / frais(m) ~ cool or fresh

froid(e) ~ cold

chaud(e) ~ warm

très chaud(e) ~ hot

Cooking

bouillon ~ bouillon, stock, broth or light soup made from boiling vegetables, poultry or meat, and straining to retain liquid

bouillir ~ to boil

braiser ~ to braise (*braisé* ~ braised)

frit ~ fried

gratin ~ broiled or oven-baked to brown surface, usually with cheese or bread crumbs

grillé(e) ~ grilled or toasted

poêle (à la) ~ pan-fried
ragoût ~ stew
rôti ~ roast

Drinks
apéritif ~ alcoholic drink served before a meal
boire ~ to drink
bière ~ beer; bière pression ~ beer on tap
boisson ~ beverage
café ~ coffee, espresso
calvados ~ alcohol made from fermented apples
digestif ~ after-dinner alcoholic drink to aid digestion
dégustation ~ tasting
eau ~ water (e.g. *verre d'eau* ~ glass of water)
eau-de-vie ~ alcohol made from fermented fruit
infusion ~ drink flavoured with an aromatic such as a fruit or herb (tisane)
pastis ~ anise-flavoured apéritif popular in France
rosé ~ pink wine
thé ~ tea
tilleul ~ limetree, common in Provence; the blossoms are infused in hot water to make a tisane
vin blanc ~ white wine
vin rouge ~ red wine

Utensils, etc.
assiette ~ plate
batterie de cuisine ~ set of pots and pans
bol ~ bowl
bouteille ~ bottle; for wine it is generally 750 millilitres or 375 ml

carafe ~ 100-millilitre glass container used to serve water or wine in a restaurant

    ~ *demi* ~ half a carafe or 50 ml

    ~ *quart* ~ quarter of a carafe or 25 ml

casseroles ~ pots and pans

couteau ~ knife

cuiller / cuillère ~ spoon

fourchette ~ fork

pannier ~ basket used to carry goods purchased at the *marché*

plateau ~ large platter or tray

serviette ~ napkin

tasse ~ cup and saucer

verre ~ drinking glass (e.g. *une verre de bière*)

Other things

l'addition ~ the bill

bouchon ~ bottle cork

bouquet garni ~ herbs tied into a bundle to flavour soups and stews; removed after cooking

brouillade ~ scrambled eggs

champignon ~ mushroom

confit(es) ~ preserve or conserve, either sweet or savoury

confiture ~ jam or fruit preserve

escargot ~ snail

farce ~ stuffing, forcemeat (*farci* ~ stuffed)

fumé ~ smoked, cured

gelée ~ jelly

graines ~ seeds

grenouille ~ frog; *cuisses de grenouille* ~ frog legs

huile ~ oil (e.g. *huile d'olive*)

manger ~ to eat

marché ~ market

marinade ~ mixture of oil, wine, spices, etc. to flavour, moisturize or tenderize meat or fish before cooking

mesclun ~ assortment of small, wild salad leaves

miel ~ honey

morille ~ morel mushroom

mousse ~ foamy, frothy, light

nouilles ~ noodles

oeuf ~ egg

petit four ~ small fancy cake, biscuit or sweet, often using marzipan and usually served after the meal

pilaf ~ rice cooked in stock

riz ~ rice

safran ~ saffron

salade ~ salad

saveur(s) ~ flavour(s)

sec, sèche ~ dry or dried

tapeno ~ Provençal word for capers

truffe ~ truffle, a pungent underground fungus; exceptionally expensive

Some Typical Provençale Dishes

blanquette de veau ~ veal stew; can also be made with other white meats

bouillabaisse ~ various species of fish with herbs, boiled and reduced; a specialty dish along the Mediterranean in Provence; sometimes called fish soup but it is more like a stew; not to be mistaken for soupe au poisson, which does not have chunks of seafood in it

chèvre chaud ~ green salad with warmed goat cheese on top

daube ~ slow-cooked meat stew using red wine to braise;

in the Camargue area of Provence, bulls killed in the bullfighting festivals are often used for *daube*; elsewhere in Provence wild boar may be used

escargots ~ snails from the garden in garlic or parsley butter served piping hot

omelette aux truffes ~ omelette with truffles; if truffles are stored with eggs the scent and taste will infuse the eggs through the shells

pot-au-feu ~ boiled meat, beef stew—a traditional comfort food

pot-pourri ~ a mixture or medley of things

poule au pot ~ stewed chicken

salade arlésienne ~ boiled potatoes, artichoke, tomatoes, olives, herbs and anchovies on top

soupe au pistou ~ minestrone soup enhanced with a paste made from fresh basil, garlic, Parmesan cheese and olive oil

salade aux tomates ~ green salad smothered in thinly-sliced ripe tomatoes

salade niçoise ~ generally contains tuna, hard-boiled eggs, tomatoes, black olives and green beans

A Few French Desserts

crème caramel ~ caramel custard (flan)

crème brulée ~ same as flan except the caramel on top is burnt with a torch, creating a hard crust

faisselle au miel ~ very fresh goat cheese with honey drizzled on top, sometimes with bits of walnut

gâteau(x) ~ cake(s)

glace ~ ice cream

tarte tatin ~ caramelized upside-down apple tart

Markets in Provence and throughout France are morning events, and some larger centres, like Avignon and Aix-en-Provence, have more than one *marché* each week. Aix has *marchés* at Place de Verdun, Place Richelme, Cours Mirabeau and Place des Précheurs. There is a flower market in Place des Précheurs on Tuesday, Thursday and Saturday.

Monday (*lundi*)
- Bédoin
- Bollène
- Tulette

Tuesday (*mardi*)
- Mondragon
- Avignon
- Caromb
- Grignon
- Aix-en-Provence
- Vaison-la-Romaine

Wednesday (*mercredi*)
- Avignon
- Arles
- Malaucène
- Valréas
- Buis les Baronnies
- Montélimar

Thursday (*jeudi*)
- Nyons
- Cairanne
- Aix-en-Provence
- Aubignan
- Rochegude
- Orange
- Avignon

Friday (*vendredi*)
- Carpentras
- Avignon
- Taulignan
- Suze-la-Rousse
- Châteauneuf-du-Pape
- Dieulefit

Saturday (*samedi*)
- Bollène
- Avignon
- Arles
- Grillon
- Montélimar
- Richerenches
- Valréas
- Aix-en-Provence

Sunday (*dimanche*)
- Avignon
- Isle-sur-la-Sorgue
- Mirabeau
- Jonquières

Nyons

Colombet ~ 53 Place de la Libération. Traditional hotel.

Le Petit Caveau ~ 9 rue Victor Hugo. Simple local cuisine.

La Belle Epoque ~ 25 Place de la Libération. Brasserie.
Popular local spot.

Une Autre Maison ~ 45 avenue Henri Rochier. Charming
provençal hotel and restaurant.

L' Oliveraie ~ En route from Nyons to Orange. Pizzas,
salads at poolside.

Moulin Ramade ~ 7 impasse du Moulin, avenue Paul
Laurens. Olives, olive oil, tapenade.

Coopérative de Nyonsais ~ Place Olivier de Serres. Olives,
olive oil, tapenade, wines.

Near Nyons

Ferme-Auberge le Moulin du Château ~ Villeperdrix, 20
km east of Nyons. Farm fare.

La Charrette Bleue ~ Exit Les Pilles, route to Gap D94.
Excellent traditional cuisine. Restaurant.

Le Bistrot ~ Place de l'Eglise, Vinsobres. Very good French
bistrot cuisine.

Ayme Truffes ~ Domain de Bramarel, 26230 Grignan.
Offers a truffling experience.

Mohair du Moulin ~ Le Moulin, 26110 Saint-Sauveur-
Gouvernet. Mohair.

Île-sur-la-Sorgue

Chez Nane ~ 7 avenue des 4-Otages. Hidden at the back

of an antique warehouse. Casual restaurant with wonderful atmosphere next to a canal; tables under the vines.

Avignon
La Mirande ~ 4 Place de La Mirande. Gracious hotel and haute cuisine.
Le Bercail ~ Ile de la Barthelasse. Café facing Avignon. Fabulous view across the river.
La Cour du Louvre ~ 23 rue Saint Agricol. Restaurant.
Hôtel d'Europe ~ 12 Place Crillon. Exceptional hotel and restaurant.

Gigondas
L'Oustalet ~ Traditional French cuisine.

Vaison-la-Romaine
Le Brin d' Olivier ~ 4 rue du Ventoux. Restaurant. Excellent cuisine.
La Fontaine ~ In Le Beffroi Hostellerie, rue de l'Évêché, Cité Médiévale. Good restaurant, charming hotel in the old village on the hill.

Le Barroux
Les Géraniums ~ Good local fare in a pleasant setting.

Cassis
Chez Gilbert ~ The Port. Next to the fishing boats. Exceptional seafood and bouillabaisse.

Aix-en-Provence
Restaurant Chez Grand-Mère ~ 1 rue Isolette. Frog legs on

the menu.

Café Verdun ~ Place de Verdun. Good café fare under the trees on the Place.

Les Deux Garçons ~ Cours Mirabeau. Traditional French cuisine.

Mondragon

La Beaugravière ~ RN7. Haute cuisine, superb truffle menu, stunning wine cellar.

This list of addresses is not meant to be comprehensive. These are places we came to know and like. I have dropped addresses from my first book where the businesses closed or were no longer up to the earlier standard.

FURTHER READING

I am indebted to the authors of the books listed here, for they greatly enhanced my understanding and pleasure of Provence.

Fiction
The Avignon Quintet ~ Lawrence Durrell
Jean de Florette ~ Marcel Pagnol (French)
Manon des sources ~ Marcel Pagnol (French)
Le grand voyage du chat Moune et autres histoires ~ Philippe Ragueneau (French)
Le serre aux truffes ~ Pierre Sogno (French)
Any mystery by Georges Simenon

Non-Fiction
Aix-en-Provence et le pays d'Aix ~ Jean Paul Coste (French)
A Year in Provence ~ Peter Mayle; as well as his other books on Provence
Cézanne and the Provençal Table ~ Jean-Bernard Naudin
In the Footsteps of Van Gogh ~ Gilles Plazy
Judgment of Paris ~ George M. Taber
La charrette bleue ~ René Barjavel (French)
La gloire de mon père ~ Marcel Pagnol (French)
Le château de ma mère ~ Marcel Pagnol (French)
Les îles des lérins ~ Jean-Jacques Antier
Le temps des secrets ~ Marcel Pagnol (French)
Markets of Provence ~ Dixon Long
Old Provence ~ Theodore Andrea Cook
Picasso: A Biography ~ Patrick O'Brian

The Invention of the Restaurant ~ Rebecca L. Spang
The Judgement of Paris ~ Ross King
Two Towns in Provence ~ M.F.K Fisher
Van Gogh: The Life ~ Steven Naifeh and Gregory White Smith
Village in the Vaucluse ~ Laurence Wylie

Food and Wine
Adventures on the Wine Route ~ Kermit Lynch
Chez Nous ~ Lydie Marshall *(provençale* cooking)
Cooking School Provence ~ Guy Gedda and Marie-Pierre Moine
French Cheeses ~ Kazuko Masui and Tomoko Yamada
Le livre de la truffe ~ Bernard Duc-Maugé and Bernard Duplessy (French)
Oz Clarke's Wine Atlas ~ Oz Clarke
Physiologie du goût ~ Jean Anthelme Brillat-Savarin (French)
The Art of Eating ~ M.F.K. Fisher
The Provence Cookbook ~ Patricia Wells
The Taste of France ~ Robert Freson
The World Atlas of Wine ~ Hugh Johnson and Jancis Robinson
Vins du Rhône ~ Arabella Woodrow (French)
Wines of the Rhône Valley ~ Robert M. Parker, Jr.

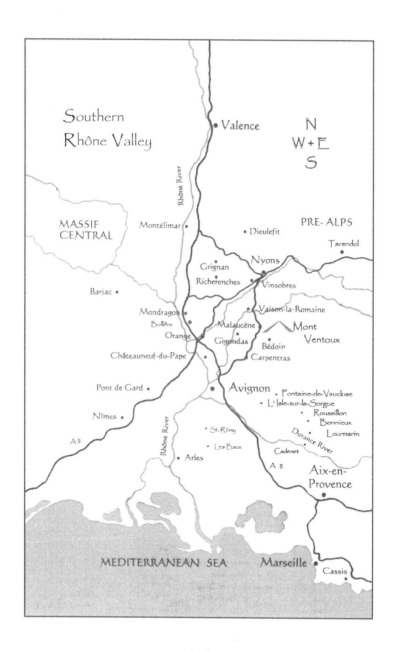

Southern
Rhône Valley

MASSIF
CENTRAL

• Valence

N
W + E
S

Rhône River

• Montélimar

• Dieulefit

PRE-ALPS

• Tarendol

• Nyons

Grignan •
Richerenches •

• Vinsobres

• Barjac

Mondragon •
Bollène •
Orange •

• Malaucène
Gigondas •

• Vaison-la-Romaine

Mont
Ventoux

• Bédoin
Carpentras

Châteauneuf-du-Pape •

Pont de Gard •

• Avignon

• Fontaine-de-Vaucluse
• L'Isle-sur-la-Sorgue
• Roussillon
• Bonnieux
• Lourmarin

Nîmes •

Rhône River

• St-Rémy

• Les Baux

Durance River

A 9

• Arles

Cadenet •

A 8

Aix-en-
Provence
•

MEDITERRANEAN SEA

Marseille •

• Cassis

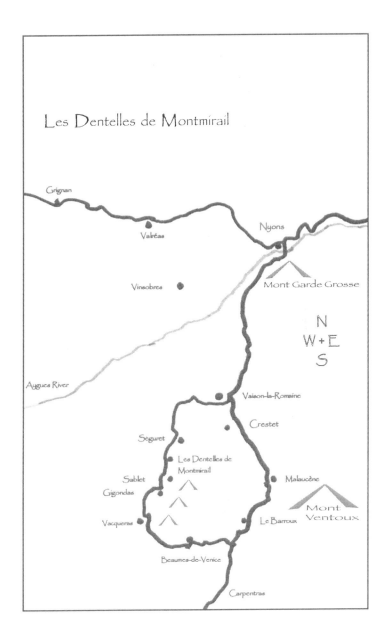

Les Dentelles de Montmirail

Grignan

Valréas

Nyons

Vinsobres

Mont Garde Grosse

N
W + E
S

Aygues River

Vaison-la-Romaine

Crestet

Séguret

Les Dentelles de
Montmirail

Sablet

Malaucène

Gigondas

Vacqueras

Le Barroux

Mont
Ventoux

Beaumes-de-Venice

Carpentras

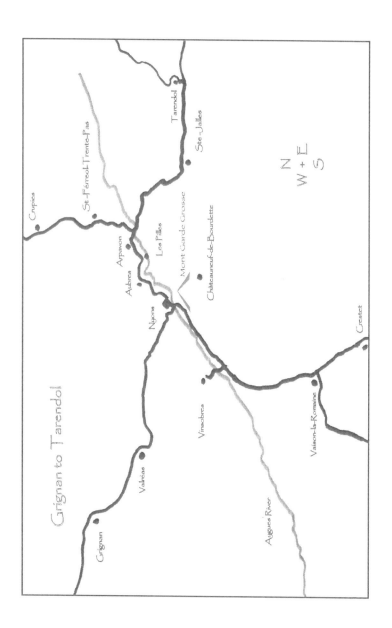

Grignan to Tarendol

Crupies
St-Ferreol-Trente-Pas
Tarendol
Ste-Jalles
Arpavon
Les Pilles
Mont Garde Grosse
Aubres
Châteauneuf-de-Bourdette
Nyons
Crestet
Vinsobres
Valréas
Vaison-la-Romaine
Grignan
Aygues River

N
W + E
S

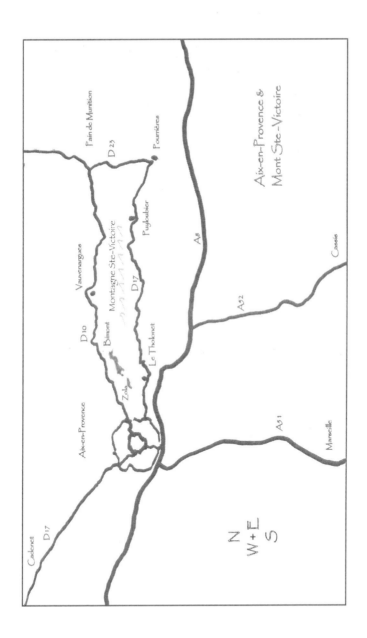

Aix-en-Provence &
Mont Ste-Victoire

221

Gordon Bitney retired from the practice of law and took up writing. This is his second book about life in Provence.

www.gordonbitney.com

Have you read . . .

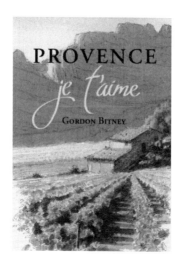

'A banshee-like cry brought us upright and awake. It was followed by confused hissing and screeching and the sounds of chaotic scrambling at the foot of the bed. Furious scratching of claws across the tiled floor and out the open door onto the balcony had us on our feet to investigate.

"They're at it again," said Marie-Hélène . . .'

'The apricots shone golden in the sun amid the green leaves. We stopped and reached up to pick a few, which we ate on the spot. Firm and luscious, their juice trickled down our fingers.'

Published by Granville Island Publishing in 2008
Also available as an ebook